Stress Cure Now

A Powerful 3-Step Plan to Cure Stress Without Medications

Freedom from Insomnia, Anxiety, Panic Attacks,
Phobias, Anger, Depression, Guilt, Psychosis,
Bipolar Affective Disorder, Attention Deficit
Disorder, Stress Eating, Addictions,
and Stress of Daily-living!

Sarfraz Zaidi, MD

Stress Cure Now
A Powerful 3-Step Plan to Cure Stress Without Medications

First Printing, January 2011

iComet Press
http://www.icometpress.com
ISBN: 978-1-4327-4810-4

Printed in the United States of America.

Disclaimer

The information in this book is true and complete to the best of our knowledge. This book is intended only as an informative guide for those wishing to know more about health issues. The information in this book is not intended to replace the advice of a health care provider. The author and publisher disclaim any liability for the decisions you make based on the information contained in this book. The information provided herein should not be used during any medical emergency or for the diagnosis and treatment of any medical condition. In no way is this book intended to replace, countermand or conflict with the advice given to by your own health care provider. The information contained in this book is general and is offered with no guarantees on the part of the author or publisher. The author and publisher disclaim all liability in connection with the use of this book. The names and identifying details of people associated with events described in this book have been changed. Any similarity to actual persons is coincidental. Any duplication or distribution of information contained herein is strictly prohibited.

iv

CONTENTS

v

STEP 1
Freedom from the Acquired Self

Q: I Can't Accept the Fact That There are so Many Bad People in the World. How Can I Not Be Angry?

STEP 2
Freedom from the Conceptual World

STEP 3
Live in the Now

xvii

Introduction

Welcome!

I am Sarfraz Zaidi, a medical doctor specializing in Diabetes and Endocrinology. As an endocrinologist, I became fully aware of the complexities of the human brain and how stress can disrupt the normal functioning of the entire hormonal system in the body. But what, really, is stress? How does it affect your body and is it possible to manage stress without medications? For years, I was intrigued by these questions.

Then one day, as I was walking in our neighborhood park pondering over these questions, I suddenly got the answers. A profound wisdom sank in. Things became crystal clear. You could call it enlightenment!

With this awakening, I felt a huge psychological load lift off my shoulders. I experienced a true psychological freedom. Now I feel a sense of joy and peace inside me which is hard to describe in words. I have much more physical and psychological energy than I ever imagined possible at the age of 55.

My outlook on life has completely changed. Now, I fully

experience every moment of life. *I truly live in the now.* I am joyful and peaceful all the time. I stay completely free of stress, even under quite stressful situations. I call it the *ultimate freedom.*

For example, four years ago, I encountered a serious illness. I lost a lot of weight and looked like someone from a concentration camp, as my wife bluntly told me one day. During this time, I was admitted to the hospital twice, but doctors still could not figure out what was wrong with me. The "old me" would have been very anxious, disappointed and depressed over this whole dreadful situation, but fortunately, this illness happened after my enlightenment. I walked on this frightening road with such a peace that even I was amazed at myself at times! Not for a moment was I depressed, disappointed, angry or anxious. Slowly, this medical situation resolved, without any medications. I believe my inner peace and energy provided immense healing power from within.

In my personal life, my wife, daughter and friends find me calmer, happier and joyful. Now I go to my clinic to truly help my patients and make a reasonable living. My memory is sharper than ever. *I don't even forget where I put my car keys anymore.* Whatever activity I am involved in, I do it better than I did before, but always with a sense of calmness and peace.

I don't create stress for myself or for anyone else! Actually, people around me feel peaceful as well. Now I have realized that true peace has a ripple effect and it starts from you.

It breaks my heart to see so many people living a stressful life and not having a clue what it's all about. That's why I was compelled to write this book. *I want to share my experience and wisdom with you. Wisdom is power. By using this power of wisdom, you can be free of your stress, right now.* Yes, it is that simple!

In "Stress Cure Now," I show you the path to the ultimate freedom from stress. Walk on this path and you can be free of stress as well. My path to a stress-free life is based on *logic,* the most powerful tool we humans have. When I examined my life, using logic, I was in for a big surprise! My whole outlook about life changed dramatically. It's as if I *woke up* from a deep psychological sleep. After this *awakening,* everything became crystal clear about:

> *The origin of stress*
> *The dynamics of stress*
> *The solution of stress*

In this book, I will share with you my earnest and sincere observations about life. I'm not trying to convince you. In no way I am trying to upset anyone's feelings. *What I describe are my observations based upon logic.* I am not judging or criticizing anyone, or any group of people. I do not have any affiliation with any political party or religious organization. You may or may not agree with me, but please think; and think logically with an open-mind. After all, it is your life. I am simply inviting you to take a fresh look at it with logic.

In order to get the most benefits out of this book, you need to read it in its *entirety*. While reading the book, you may find your mind popping with questions, judging some parts of the book to be right, exciting and interesting while others as wrong, boring and repetitive. It's all fine. Just do yourself a favor and keep reading the book with an open mind. Write down your questions. Most likely you will find answers in the later part of the book.

The book has been in the making over the past five years. Since my enlightenment, I would have periods of what I can describe as "spontaneous outpouring of original thoughts." I would write these down. Then I decided to compile these "episodic writings" into a book form. The book went through only *minimal* editing, because I wanted to keep the *original* thoughts intact. That's why the book does not follow the strict rules of "book writing."

Lastly, a word of caution. Please do not stop taking any medications on your own. You need to discuss it with your physician. In no way I am trying to diagnose or treat your medical or psychiatric condition.

I am simply showing you a new way to "cure stress" and live a "stress-free life."

Chapter 1

The Harmful Effects of Stress

Stress affects your emotional as well as physical health. There is a strong mind - body connection. The Mind controls the function of each and every cell in the body. *A stressed out mind leads to a stressed out body.*

Stress, in this way, plays an important role in the causation of most medical illnesses. Of course, stress is not the only culprit. There are other factors such as genetics, nutrition, lifestyle, pollution and micro-organisms that take part in the development of medical illnesses. But stress is a major player.

Here are some examples how stress adversely affects your health:

Stress Causes High Blood Pressure

Stress is a well known risk factor for high blood pressure. In my office, if your blood pressure is found to be elevated, I'll give you my brief talk (a glimpse of what is in this book) and check your blood pressure again in about 30 minutes. It often comes down by 10-20 points. Patients are amazed.

Some patients say, "But I'm in your office, doc. That's why my blood pressure is high." Well, it is true that just being in a physician's office can be stressful and stress does raise your blood pressure through the mind-body connection.

Now imagine how frequently you deal with stress in daily life: someone cuts you off in traffic; your boss cancels your vacation; your child misbehaves in front of the school principal; your spouse doesn't listen to what you say; your son calls you for more money. You got the picture?

The fact is that life is full of annoyances and of course, you don't keep checking blood pressure all the time. In many people, these stresses of daily life trigger a rise in blood pressure. Initially, your blood pressure goes up and then comes down. That's called *labile hypertension*. After a few years of these spikes, your blood pressure remains elevated all the time. Then, you're diagnosed with *"hypertension"* and your physician typically prescribes medications, all without paying any attention to the root cause: *stress*. In time, you'll need more and more medications to control your hypertension, as the root cause remains untreated.

When patients consult me, they're usually already on medications to treat their hypertension. Instead of adding another pill to control their blood pressure, I teach them what you are about to learn in this book and this strategy works extremely well. In medical literature, there's abundant evidence to show that techniques which utilize the mind-body connection can successfully lower blood pressure.

Stress Causes Heart Attacks

Acute stress can lead to an actual heart attack. I'm not

talking about just a sensation of chest tightness while you're under stress (which often turns out not to be an actual heart attack). I'm referring to an actual heart attack verified by ECG and blood testing. This association between stress and heart attack is very well documented in medical literature and my extensive medical experience testifies to it.

I vividly remember one particular case. I was watching the final basketball championship game between the Los Angeles Lakers and the Detroit Pistons on TV in 1988, while on call in a Detroit hospital. The Pistons lost in the last few seconds of the game. Being a big Pistons fan, it broke my heart. While talking to my friends about our collective agony, I got an emergency call from the nurse. A heart patient who was watching the game actually suffered another heart attack after watching his team lose the playoff! This is the power of stress.

Stress Causes Infections

We are constantly exposed to viruses and bacteria, but we don't develop infections all the time. The reason? Our immune system, which is there to recognize the offending agent, mounts an attack and kills it.

When your immune system is healthy, it gets rid of the offending virus or bacteria so fast that you don't even develop any symptoms. On the other hand, if your immune system is weak, the offending virus or bacteria can thrive and results into frequent and prolonged illnesses that can even kill a person.

Stress is a major reason for weakening of your immune system. Consequently, it increases your risk for all sorts of infections, such as common colds, flu, bronchitis, pneumonia, tuberculosis and other infections.

Stress Causes Autoimmune Diseases

In an autoimmune disease, your immune system goes haywire. It starts to attack and kill your own cells as if they are alien and therefore, must be destroyed. But why does the immune system go crazy?

While there are many reasons for the dysfunction of the immune system, *stress reeks havoc on the immune system* and therefore, plays a major role in the development of auto-immune diseases.

Some examples of autoimmune diseases:
- Asthma
- Eczema
- Ulcerative colitis
- Crohns' disease
- Irritable bowel syndrome
- Peptic ulcer disease
- Vitamin B12 deficiency
- Pernicious anemia
- Type 1 diabetes

- Multiple sclerosis (M.S.)
- Chronic rheumatologic conditions (such as rheumatoid arthritis, fibromyalgia, systemic lupus erythematosis, commonly known as lupus, and ankylosing spondylitis).
- Autoimmune thyroid disease, which can either cause you to have a *low* level of thyroid hormone (Hashimoto's thyroiditis) or a *high* level of thyroid hormone (Graves' disease).

As an endocrinologist, I see a lot of patients with autoimmune Type 1 diabetes and autoimmune thyroid diseases such as Over-active thyroid (Graves' disease) and Under-active thyroid (Hashimoto's thyroiditis). These patients often also have other autoimmune diseases listed above.

In these patients, I consistently find a high level of stress, usually a Type A personality (overachiever) and a lot of anxiety. In addition, these patients are also low in Vitamin D.

I vividly remember one particular case: *A young female came to see me for an over-active thyroid condition (Graves' disease). She was accompanied by her husband. During my first encounter, I found that her husband answered all of my questions. I didn't make much of it and thought that she was probably a shy person. I started her on a drug to treat Graves' disease.*

A month later, on the second appointment, she was accompanied not only by her husband, but her five children. Her husband introduced each child, one by one. When he uttered their name, each child would stand up, step forward, say their name and sit down (only after being told to do so). Somehow, it reminded me of the movie, "The Sound of Music" when the Von Trapp children introduce themselves with an almost military precision. Anyway, I thought this family was a bit odd, but didn't think much beyond that. I refilled the patient's medicine and advised her to see me again in two months with a repeat blood test. I did stress that the drug she was taking can cause serious side-effects, so close monitoring was important.

Unfortunately, she did not show up for her next appointment. I got concerned and tried to contact her by telephone and letters, but to no avail. I kept thinking that without the medicine, she would develop severe symptoms of overactive thyroid and end up in the emergency department of a hospital.

Finally, one day she showed up in my office after about a year all by herself. During this visit, she couldn't stop talking. She was fluent in English and not shy at all.

She started by saying that her husband had passed away. "How do you feel?" I asked. "Oh! I'm feeling just fine. I haven't taken the medicine you prescribed for nine months, but I feel no symptoms of over-active thyroid." Then she also explained that her husband was extremely suspicious of her, kept her inside the house and was a control freak. She had been *very afraid of him. She said her life was a "living hell on earth."*

I went ahead and ordered a blood test to check her thyroid hormone level which, to my utter astonishment, turned out to be perfectly normal. To put things in perspective, Graves' disease usually requires treatment with drugs for about two years with a success rate of about 50%. The alternative treatment is an ablation with radioactive iodine. It does not subside by itself in a matter of months. It is unheard of. And yet, that is what happened when the stress in her life disappeared. This case clearly illustrates the power of stress in causing Graves' disease, an autoimmune disorder.

Stress Causes Diabetes

While there are several factors that contribute to the development of diabetes, stress is an important one.

This is how:

Type 2 Diabetes:

About 95% of diabetics suffer from Type 2 diabetes, which occurs due to a process in the body called *insulin resistance*. Stress is a major cause for insulin resistance. Obesity is another important culprit for insulin resistance. Stress through *Stress Eating* plays the main underlying cause for obesity. In this way, stress significantly contributes to a person's obesity and risk for developing diabetes.

7

Insulin resistance is a process in the body which causes insulin, a chemical in your body, to be less effective in keeping your blood sugar normal. Consequently, your body produces more insulin in order to keep your blood sugar normal. This compensatory increase in the amount of insulin may control your blood sugar for a while, but it's harmful for the rest of the body. Large amounts of insulin can raise your *blood pressure* and increase your risk for *cancer*. Insulin resistance also increases your risk for *heart attacks* and *strokes*.

After many years of escalating insulin resistance, eventually your insulin producing cells in the pancreas get exhausted and cannot churn out the huge amounts of insulin needed to keep your blood sugar normal. At this point, your blood sugar starts to rise and you end up being diagnosed with Type 2 diabetes.

Type 1 Diabetes:

Type I diabetes is the other type of diabetes. It is much less common, accounting for about 5% of diabetics. Type 1 diabetes is an autoimmune disease in which your *dysfunctional* immune system starts to attack and kill your own insulin producing cells. Eventually your pancreas is unable to produce any insulin and you become diabetic. As I mentioned earlier, stress is a major reason for the dysfunction of your immune system. To learn more about diabetes, please refer to my book, "*Take Charge of Your Diabetes.*"

8

Stress Worsens Diabetes.

Many diabetics know that their blood glucose gets elevated when they are under stress, even though their eating habits didn't change at all. They also know that with the release of stress, their elevated blood glucose comes down.

Over the years, I have seen many such examples. I vividly remember one particular case.

The gentleman was a highly successful businessman who was struggling to keep his blood glucose levels down. Then he went on a vacation to his native homeland in a rural setting. When he came back from vacation, he came to see me. "Doc, you've been telling me about the effects of stress on diabetes. You are absolutely right. During my vacation, my blood glucose readings were perfect for the first time. Now that I'm back at work, my blood glucose levels are going up again." He was genuinely excited to see for himself the strong relationship between stress and high blood glucose levels.

Even subtle stress can elevate your blood glucose levels. For example, some diabetics get so preoccupied by their blood glucose readings that they stress themselves out. As a result, their blood glucose reading starts to escalate. Then they get more stressed out and a vicious cycle sets in.

I remember one lady who was always preoccupied with

9

her blood glucose readings. During one visit, I told her to stop checking her blood glucose. Two months later, her diabetes was under better control, as evidenced by her blood test report from the laboratory. She was completely amazed.

These examples clearly demonstrate the negative impact of stress on diabetes.

Stress Causes Chronic Diarrhea and Constipation

Millions of people suffer from chronic diarrhea and/or constipation. Often these symptoms are accompanied by abdominal cramps, excessive gas and tiredness. In medical terms, we call it Irritable Bowel Syndrome (IBS).

Stress is a well known major factor for IBS. Most people who suffer from IBS can clearly relate their bout of diarrhea or constipation to an acute stress.

In a more severe form, people also develop blood and mucus in their loose stools. This condition is medically known as Inflammatory Bowel Disease (IBD). Ulcerative colitis and Crohn's disease are two forms of IBD. Stress is a very well known risk factor for IBD.

Stress Causes Low Back Pain

Millions of people suffer from chronic low back pain which is often debilitating and interferes with their lifestyle. They visit their doctor who often prescribes pain killers and orders a CT or MRI scan which often shows some degenerative abnormalities in the spine. Then physicians and patients conveniently blame these structural abnormalities for their symptoms. But here are some interesting medical facts.

Many people, while having some chronic degenerative changes in their spine, do not suffer from chronic back pain while others do. Several studies have clearly shown that the psychological make-up of a person is the principal determinant whether a person will suffer from chronic back pain or not.

I have often seen patients who develop severe back pain when under severe psychological stress. And when the acute stress is gone, so is their back pain.

I am not discounting cases of severe back pain which are due to structural changes, such as fracture of a vertebra or acute prolapse of a disc. However, these pains actually subside after a few weeks. Chronic back pain that goes on for months and years is at least, in part, due to stress. Furthermore, chronic debilitating back pain itself creates more stress, which further worsens back pain and in this way, a vicious cycle sets in.

Stress causes spasms of muscles in the back and contributes to ongoing back pain months after a vertebra or a prolapsed disc has healed. Vitamin D deficiency is another common cause of chronic back pain, which unfortunately remains undiagnosed and untreated in most people.

11

Stress Causes Cancer

While there are many factors that can cause cancer, stress is one of them.

A normal immune system is important for killing abnormal cells in the body, including cancer cells. This function is carried out by specialized cells, called Natural Killer cells. That's why a normal functioning immune system is your safety net against cancer.

Stress impairs your immune system and thus may increase your risk for cancer. And if you get diagnosed with cancer, you are completely devastated. The amount of stress is unbelievable, which further impairs the ability of your own immune system to kill cancer cells.

Stress Can Halt Your Menses

In women, stress is well known to cause a cessation of menses. Acute emotional trauma, such as a divorce, preparing for a performance or an examination, or a young girl leaving home for the first time to go to college, can stop menses for a while.

Severe emotional stress affects the hypothalamus, a vital structure in the brain, which then affects the ovaries in such a way that menses come to a halt. It is body's way to stop reproduction at the time of stress.

Stress Causes Impotence, Decreased Libido and Infertility

Stress is a major reason for impotence, lack of sexual drive and decreased fertility due to a decrease in sex hormones. Again, it is the body's way to stop reproduction at a time of stress.

Ironically, when people develop these symptoms, they get more stressed out, which leads to worsening of the symptoms and a vicious cycle sets in.

Stress Causes Chronic Headaches

Chronic headaches are often the result of underlying chronic stress. Due to stress, the muscles around the skull get tense and give rise to a headache. In medical terms, we refer to them as *tension headaches*. Ironically, we treat them with medicines without paying any attention to the underlying cause – stress. Amazing!

Stress Causes Memory Loss

Stress is a major cause for memory loss. Find out for yourself. Next time you're upset, you'll notice that your memory is not very sharp. In fact, people who stay upset and angry often end up with memory loss as they grow older, as compared to people who are the happy go lucky type. Because physicians cannot find a treatable medical reason for their memory loss, they

13

label this condition as Alzheimer's disease. The news of this diagnosis creates huge anxiety for patients as well as caregivers. Many people these days worry that they will develop Alzheimer's disease in their old age. In this way, they hasten their own memory loss, while worrying about how to prevent memory loss. How ironic!

Stress Causes Psychological Illnesses

Stress is the major reason for insomnia, anxiety, panic attacks, depression, bipolar affective disorder, attention deficit disorder, post-traumatic stress disorder, phobias, addictions and even psychosis. I discuss these disorders in detail later in the book.

Stress Causes Tiredness

Tiredness is perhaps the most common symptom people experience. Often, it's caused by a mixture of psychological and physical effects of stress. *A stressed out mind leads to a stressed out body.*

The following effects of stress can contribute to tiredness in a person. For many people, more than one condition is a causative factor of tiredness.

- Continuous psychological pressure wears you down. It could be pressure to achieve, succeed or accomplish. The pressure could arise out of

14

performing, seeking approval or meeting certain tight schedules or deadlines.

- Insomnia, which causes daytime somnolence and tiredness.
- Depression leads to low energy state.
- Autoimmune thyroid disease (underactive or overactive thyroid) causes tiredness.
- Diabetes, if uncontrolled, leads to tiredness.
- Vitamin B12 deficiency, which is an autoimmune disorder, causes tiredness.
- Chronic rheumatologic conditions such as rheumatoid arthritis and lupus are due to autoimmune dysfunction and give rise to a lot of tiredness.
- Adrenal Insufficiency: A rare condition in which your immune system attacks and kills your adrenal glands. You end up with profound fatigue and low blood pressure.

In summary, stress working through the mind-body connection plays a pivotal role in causing most illnesses. Obviously, it's important to understand the mind-body connection. In the next chapter, let's take a close look at it.

Chapter 2

The Mind-Body Connection

In order to fully understand how stress causes physical and psychological ailments, we first need to understand the *Mind-Body connection.*

The brain controls the function of each and every cell in the body. At the same time, it continuously gets feedback from each and every cell in the body. *It's a two-way traffic!*

The brain and body are intimately connected to each other through three main mechanisms: *Nerve fibers, Hormones and the Immune system.*

1. Nerve Fibers

Nerve fibers are basically an extension of the brain. There is a vast network of nerve fibers in our body. Some of these nerves carry information from the brain to the body and other types of nerves carry information from the body to the brain.

For example, when you move your hand, what happens behind the scene works like this: The brain sends information through the nerves to a group of muscles in the hand. Some of these muscles contract and other relax in a harmony, resulting in

17

a certain type of movement. These types of actions are called *voluntary actions* and the nerve fibers that carry these actions constitute the *somatic nervous system.*

Stress Affects the Somatic Nervous System

Normally, somatic nerves keep a certain level of tone in the muscles. Under stress, this tone is markedly increased, giving rise to *tense muscles.* Often, we are unaware of this tension, but if we pay attention, we can easily sense this tension.

For example, right now, take a break from reading this book and pay attention to your muscles. Relax your muscles. Only after you're relaxed, will you realize how tense your muscles were before.

Tense muscles are the main reason for chronic headaches, chronic low back pain and other aches and pains that so many people suffer from. For the same reason, it feels good after someone gives you a massage.

The Autonomic Nervous System

Then there are *involuntary actions*, such as the beating of the heart or the act of breathing. These actions take place continuously and most of the time we're not even aware of them. That's why we call them involuntary actions. These actions are carried out by a specialized type of nerves called *autonomic nerves.*

18

Autonomic nerves control the *automatic* functioning of our internal organs such as the beating of the heart, inhalation and exhalation of air, production of saliva and digestive juices from the stomach and motility of the intestines.

The autonomic nervous system is divided into two types: the *Sympathetic Nervous System* and the *Parasympathetic Nervous System.* Both of these systems are extremely important for the normal functioning of our body.

The Sympathetic nervous system is the predominant player during exercise and "threatening conditions." Sympathetic nerves carry out their function by producing two chemicals: *Adrenaline* and *nor-adrenaline.* These chemicals instantaneously increase your heart rate and blood pressure, dilate your airways for optimal breathing, increase your blood glucose, make your pupils dilate and make changes in your lens to optimize distance vision. In this way, the sympathetic nervous system primes your body to face a threatening condition and prepares you to either fight or run away. That's why we call it the "fight-or-flight" response. The activated sympathetic nervous system also acts on the skin and causes increased sweating and goose bumps.

The Parasympathetic Nervous System, on the other hand, is the predominant player during resting conditions and after eating. These nerves act by producing a chemical called *Acetylcholine.* This chemical causes an instantaneous increase in the amount of saliva and digestive juices from the stomach, pancreas, gall bladder and intestines. It also increases motility of the stomach, intestines and urinary bladder. It increases insulin production from the pancreas to store excess calories from food into the muscles and fat. In addition, it decreases your heart rate. In this way, the parasympathetic nervous system works to digest food, store food energy and also to conserve energy by decreasing its expenditure.

Stress Affects the Autonomic Nervous System

Stress disrupts the normal functioning of the autonomic nervous system and causes a variety of symptoms. Chronic stress, for example, causes an increased release of nor-adrenaline which causes an increase in *blood pressure*.

Acute stress can cause a sudden rush of adrenaline and nor-adrenaline which causes the heart to beat faster and more forcefully. It can precipitate an *acute heart attack* if someone already has a diseased heart.

Chronic stress disrupts the normal functioning of the parasympathetic nervous system and can give rise to chronic diarrhea and abdominal cramping, typically seen in patients with Irritable Bowel Syndrome.

2. Hormones

In addition to nerves, the body and brain are also connected through *hormones*.

20

What is a hormone? Simply put, a hormone is a substance produced by one part of the body that then gets in blood circulation and affects the functions of various organs in the body. For example, thyroid hormone is produced by the thyroid gland in your neck. Then it gets in blood circulation and exerts its affects on almost every organ in the body.

How much thyroid hormone is produced at any given time is regulated by a tiny structure in the brain, the *Pituitary gland*, which itself is controlled by another tiny structure in the brain, the *Hypothalamus.*

Not only thyroid hormone, but most other hormones in the body such as testosterone, estrogen, cortisol and growth hormone, are tightly regulated by the hypothalamus. Therefore, you could call the hypothalamus the "high command center" for most hormones in the body.

Now consider this: The hypothalamus is connected to various parts of the brain, including the brain centers for our memory and emotions, known as the Hippocampus, Amygdala and Prefrontal cortex.

Emotional stress can alter your hormones working through the hypothalamus and cause symptoms such as cessation of menses, impotence and decreased fertility.

Adrenal Glands

By far the most important stress hormones are produced by your adrenal glands, two tiny glands that each sit on top of each kidney. These stress hormones are cortisol, adrenaline and nor-adrenaline.

Stress, working through the prefrontal cortex-hippocampus-amygdala, the hypothalamus and the pituitary gland, ultimately makes your adrenal glands pour out large amounts of cortisol.

A high level of cortisol worsens insulin resistance, weakens muscles, causes obesity, raises blood pressure and blood glucose, weakens bones and impairs the immune system.

In addition to cortisol, the adrenal glands also produce adrenaline and nor-adrenaline which get into blood circulation and cause all the effects discussed earlier under "Fight or flight" response. In fact, the adrenaline and nor-adrenaline released from the adrenal glands stay in blood circulation for a much longer period as compared to these chemicals produced by the sympathetic nerve fibers at their nerve endings.

Stress, especially in the form of *worries* and *anxiety,* provokes a "fight-or-flight" response and can give rise to symptoms of *panic attacks* such as palpitations, sweating, hyperventilation, chest tightness and headache.

When activated on a chronic basis by worries and

anxiety, this "fight-or-flight" response contributes to palpitations, sweaty palms (or even generalized increased sweating), high blood pressure, high blood glucose, chronic headaches and a constant rushed feeling which is quite exhausting.

Renin-Angiotensin-Aldosterone System (RAAS).

There is another very important hormonal system in the body called the Renin-Angiotensin-Aldosterone System (RAAS). This system helps to maintain our blood pressure.

Sympathetic nerves stimulate RAAS. Overactive sympathetic nerves due to stress cause over-stimulation of RAAS which results in high blood pressure.

3. Immune System

Lymphocytes are the principal cells of the immune system. Stress causes an increased production of cortisol, which has deleterious affects on these cells. Cortisol can kill lymphocytes, including the natural-killer (NK) cells. Remember, NK cells are important in getting rid of cancer cells naturally. In this way, stress reduces your ability to get rid of cancer cells.

Cortisol also impairs the function of the lymphocytes and increases your risk for infections.

Lymphocytes produce a number of chemicals (such as interferon, interleukins) which then get into blood circulation and

23

have a wide range of actions on various parts of the body. It is interesting to note that some of these products of lymphocytes can stimulate the hypothalamus which ultimately leads to an increased production of cortisol. In this way, a vicious cycle sets in.

In conclusion, perhaps now you understand why the mind and body are so closely connected. They essentially work as one unit. It's one example of the intelligence residing in your body. You are born with it. You don't learn it in school. We could call it *universal intelligence*, because it is present in each and every living being.

Disruption of any part of this unit leads to a widespread dysfunction. Stress disrupts the harmonious functioning of this unit through several mechanisms, leading to a variety of clinical signs and symptoms we call diseases.

Chapter 3

What is Stress?

You are finally home after a long day at work. It's time to relax. You ease yourself into your new sofa. Without even realizing it, soon your mind is back at work. You think about how your day went: that annoying customer; the ungrateful, greedy boss; the jealous, selfish co-worker.

Finally, your husband arrives exhausted and complaining about all of the annoyances he went through during the day. He also expresses his worries about the bleak economic future for the family.

On the answering machine, you hear a reminder about your appointment the next day with your doctor to discuss the result of your biopsy. What if the biopsy turns out to be cancerous? A wave of shivers runs through your body. In bed, you toss and turn but sleep is miles away. At 2 am, you pop some sleeping pills and manage to get four hours of sleep.

At the physician's office your biopsy report is fine, but your weight is up, blood pressure is high and your blood sugar is also borderline high. Later, on the way back to work, you can't help but think about your dad, who couldn't walk in his old age due to a stroke caused by his high blood pressure and your mom, who lost her eyesight because of diabetes.

Suddenly, you feel your heart pounding, chest tightening, and body losing all of its strength. Next, you wake up in the emergency room at a hospital ....

The Stress of daily living has horrendous consequences. Everyone suffers from it to a certain degree. People reluctantly accept it. "This is part of life and there's nothing you can do about it." In this way, they rationalize their stressful living.

Is it possible to be free of stress? Don't you need to fully understand stress before you can be free of it? Stress comes in many forms. For the sake of discussion, I divide stress into two types:

- Outer stress
- Inner Stress

Outer Stress

Outer stress is what we generally refer to when we talk of stress. This is the stress due to an external factor, often out of our control, such as loss of a loved one, losing a job, missing a flight.

These are basically situations which keep happening, one after another. There are brief periods when we get some relief. You may think, "Ah! Finally I have no stress," but before you know it, some other stressful situation arrives.

For example, after years of hard work, you finally have the ideal job you always wanted. You have a nice house, a nice car and a wonderful family. Then one day, you have a serious car accident and spend the next several weeks on crutches. Finally, you're back at work, but find out that your company is in financial trouble. Soon, you're laid off. Lack of a job, obviously, creates a huge stress. A few months later, your wife is diagnosed with cancer. While she's undergoing chemotherapy, you find out you need heart bypass surgery. In the meantime, your teenager is having problems with teachers. You find yourself a frequent visitor to the principal's office.

Another example: You finally reach the retirement that you've been dreaming of for years. Soon after retirement, you discover that you have prostate cancer, for which you undergo surgery. As a complication of surgery, you can no longer control your urine. A few months later, your wife falls, breaks her hip and ends up in the hospital. In the meantime, your daughter calls to let you know that she is going through a divorce and will need financial aid from you.

Well, you get the idea of the many types of outer stresses that we encounter in our lives!

Inner Stress

Inner stress, on the other hand, is a different animal. It's there all the time. With few exceptions, everyone is suffering from it. It stays with you wherever you go.

What is this inner stress? It's the feeling of restlessness, agitation, emptiness, worthlessness, sadness, boredom, frustrations, annoyances, anger, hate, jealousy, guilt, fear, nervousness and anxiety.

Where does this inner stress come from? If you pay close attention, you'll find that this inner stress comes from your own *inner voice*, the voice in your head that never stops even though you have nothing to solve. Often you're completely unaware of it. It's like your mind is on *autopilot*.

Some Examples:

- You're home after work. Now's the time to relax, but your mind keeps replaying all that happened at work: the demanding customers, the selfish boss, the insensitive co-workers.

- You find yourself criticizing others even though you're sitting alone.

- You're still trying to win the argument you had with your spouse, a week ago… in your head.

- You experience a low level of irritability when there is no

28

obvious reason for it.

- You think to yourself: "No one, even my spouse, understands me. No one really cares about me. They're all only interested in my money."

- You feel the urge to keep doing something, even if you're on a vacation and supposed to be relaxing.

- You push yourself constantly, even though you have many accomplishments. You feel like you're in the race all the time and you have to win at all costs.

- You feel dissatisfied and bored with your apparently successful life.

- You become agitated over some political or social issue. Reading a newspaper or watching the news makes you angry at the world.

- No one understands your point of view, but you think you could save the world if all the morons out there would only listen to you!

- You're on vacation but find yourself complaining about the flight, the hotel, the food, the weather, the beach, the people, etc.

- You feel low and depressed even though you have everything going for you.

- You feel rushed and tired all the time without any medical reason for it.

- You're afraid of losing your job, your health, your looks, your possessions, your respect, your fame, your credibility.

- You're afraid of losing planet Earth. The destruction of mankind is looming.

- You're afraid that you may fail as a parent or a spouse. You feel you may not be able to fulfill all responsibilities at home, at work or in society at large. You're afraid of being a failure.

- You're sad because you've been a failure in life. You have nothing to show for all your struggles to succeed.

- You're furious because life has been so unfair to you.

- You're furious at publishers for not accepting your wonderful manuscript.

- You're mad at your mother, father, unfaithful spouse, insincere friends or elementary school teacher.

30

- You're mad at the teenagers of today. You believe the world is coming to an end.

- You hope for a better future.

- You feel lucky to live in a particular city and a particular country and deep down, you're afraid that one day, you may lose your paradise.

- You love your glorious past (because the present does not appear to be so good).

- You want to change the world the way you want (because you're dissatisfied with how things are at this moment).

- You're angry at people who look a certain way as well as those who belong to certain religions or political parties you disapprove of.

- Complaining is your favorite pastime.

- You wish the world was a better place.

- You feel frustrated you can't kick your habits of excessive eating, smoking, drinking or shopping even though intellectually, you understand their harmfulness.

31

- You hear a nagging voice in your head saying you're not good enough, you're lazy, you're a loser, you'll be late again or you'll embarrass yourself.

- You often hear these kind of nagging voices in your head: *what if, what will I, what may, this should not have happened, or why didn't this happen, why didn't I, why did I....*

- You're mad at yourself. "How could I be so selfish, deceitful, immoral, dishonest...."

Who is this *inner voice* that torments you and creates all of your inner stress, even when there's no stressful situation? If we could figure this out, if we could get to the root of it, then we could do something about it, right?

Chapter 4

The Root Cause of Stress

After clearly seeing the relationship between stress and physical as well as psychological illness, I started a journey to figure out the *root cause of stress.*

I wondered, "When I get stressed out, who is this "*I*" inside me who gets stressed out? Who am *I* in reality?"

Do you Know Who You Are?

And I ask you the same question. Who is this "*I*" inside you who gets stressed out? Who are you in reality?" Do you know who you are?

Most people reply by saying," I am Mr. So and So. I am a doctor, an engineer, a publisher, a teacher, etc. I am a father, a husband, an American, an Italian, a Canadian, etc. But are you really who you think you are?

In order to figure out *who I am not* and *who I really am,* I used logic. As a true scientist, I wanted to find the answer myself without any preconceived notions. Let me first clarify what I mean when I use the word "logic." To me, logic means simple common sense. You are born with it, you don't go to school to learn it. It is not intellectualization, rationalization or reasoning.

And then, one day, I suddenly woke up from my deep psychological sleep! Let me share with you my own journey to Awakening.

My Personal Awakening!

Using logic, I realized that I was still me before I became a doctor, bought a house and owned a car. I was still me before I became a father and before I became a husband. I was still me before I went to medical school, college and high school. And I was still me before I started elementary school. I was still me before I started talking, walking, standing, crawling and sitting. And I was still me when I was born… So I was me, the real me when I was born and everything else, I acquired later on in life.

With this realization, a shocking sensation went through my body. Then suddenly, there was a relief, as if a huge load was lifted off my shoulders. Then, there was a feeling of inner peace, freedom and joy. And I have enjoyed this feeling in varying degrees ever since.

It is such a logical truth that it needs no argument and no validation. *I had found the real Me*: The true, original Me, the one that I was born with. I call it the true, *original self.* And then I acquired another self as I grew up. I call it the *Acquired Self.*

You, me and every other human on the planet is born with the original, true self and later on, acquires another self, the Acquired Self. Let's take a closer look at these two psychological selves.

The True, Original Self

In order to know your true, original self, observe little babies, just a day or so old. I had the opportunity to be in charge of a well baby nursery in my early career as a doctor and observed about sixty babies every day. Later, I had the wonderful experience of having my own baby.

When I observe little babies, I see that as soon as their basic physical needs are met (i.e. a full stomach, a clean diaper and a warm blanket), they are *joyful* from within! They smile and go to sleep. Once their stomach is full, they don't want any more food. If you were to force more food than they need, they would regurgitate. They eat to satisfy their hunger and that's all. *Wanting more* does not exist and that's why they are so *content*. You could feed them breast milk, cow's milk or formula. To them, it doesn't matter as long as it agrees with their stomach and satisfies their hunger.

They don't say "I don't like your milk, Mom. I like formula milk better." You won't hear, "Mom, you wrapped me in a pink blanket with butterflies on it. I'm a boy. Therefore, I need a blue blanket with pictures of dinosaurs on it."
Likes and dislikes do not exist. *Concepts* do not exist.

35

There are no *preferences or judgments*. No *embarrassment or shame*. They are *simply practical*.

They have no *past* or *future*. They are not worried if mom will be around for the next feed. If they did, they wouldn't be able to go to sleep. Because they don't think about the future, there are no *worries*. That's why they have no problem going to sleep. They are so *vulnerable* but fear remains miles away. There is total *lack of control*, but no fear whatsoever. They are happy just looking around. They truly *live in the moment*.

The mind is not yet spoiled by conditioning. They don't like or dislike someone because of his color, religion, nationality or wealth. It's because they have not acquired any *concepts* about religion, nationality, history or money.

No wanting more, no likes or dislikes, no preferences, no prejudices, no fear, no anger, no hate, no religion, no nationality. Just pure joy, contentment and peace. Every moment is fresh and new. *This is the true human nature.* I like to call it the "True Self," the self that you and I and everyone else on the planet is born with.

Now let's see what happens to this wonderful, joyful, peaceful and fearless human being.

The Acquired Self

Gradually, another self develops as you acquire

information, ideas, concepts, experiences and so on. This, I call the *Acquired Self.* This Acquired Self develops as a result of psychosocial conditioning. It is given to you by your parents, your school and then your society in general.

As you grow, this Acquired Self gets bigger and bigger. It gets in the driver seat, pushing the true, original self onto the passenger side and later into the back seat and eventually, into the trunk.

As a grown up, all you see is this Acquired Self. You identify with this Acquired Self. *That's who you think you are.* Your identity gets *hijacked* by the Acquired Self. Instead of seeing the hijacker for what it is, you think that's who you are. Amazing!

This Acquired Self controls your thoughts, emotions, experiences and actions. *This Acquired Self is the reason for your psychological pain and suffering which constitutes your inner stress.*

Amazingly, you are not even aware of it. Why? Because it has taken over you, like a parasite or a hijacker. You think this is who you are. I like to call it the *Monster within* because it is seemingly *powerful*, very *controlling*, *treacherous*, *cunning*, but in the end, is *virtual* and *unreal*.

This monstrous Acquired Self torments you and creates stress even when there is no stressful situation. In life, sooner or later, you are faced with a stressful situation - what I call *outer*

37

stress. Already up to your neck with your *inner stress*, you over-react to *outer stress*, the stressful situation, and that makes it worse.

Sadly, you don't even have a clue what's going on, because you completely identify with the monstrous Acquired Self, the mastermind behind all of your stress. What an irony! You could call it the *enemy within*.

Sadly, you're completely out of touch with your true self: the source of true joy, contentment and inner peace. In the total grip of the monstrous Acquired Self, you suffer and suffer and create stress not only for yourself, but for others as well.

Please be aware that I am using the terms hijacker, parasite, monster and enemy simply to communicate. I use these terms without attaching any *negativity* to them.

Chapter 5

How You Acquire the "Acquired Self"

The Acquired Self within you is very complex, has many layers and keeps getting bigger and bigger every day. In order to understand this very convoluted monstrous, Acquired Self, you need to take a close look at its composition and its making.

Your Acquired Self primarily consists of thoughts and emotions. With every thought, there is an emotion attached. The bundles of thought and emotion constitute your Acquired Self, the monster within.

The composition of the Acquired Self varies from person to person depending upon his/her unique environment and upbringing. However, its main features are more or less the same, as will become evident as we proceed in this book.

The architect at the root of making and feeding your Acquired Self is your society, which itself is a *Collective Acquired Self*. Let's call this Collective Acquired Self the *Society Monster,* just for the sake of description. (It is not my intention to attach any negativity to the Collective Acquired Self.)

Think of the monster within you as an offspring of the Society Monster. Your Monster is produced by the Society

39

Monster and depends on its constant feeding to get stronger. The Society Monster works through your parents, school, books, news media, movies and society in general.

There are three mechanisms responsible for creating your monstrous Acquired Self:

- Psychosocial conditioning.
- Instillation of information.
- Creation of past and future.

In the next three chapters, we'll take a close look at each one of these mechanisms.

Chapter 6

Psychosocial Conditioning

Psychosocial conditioning plays a major part in creating your Acquired Self. It starts at home. Parents and grandparents play their role to condition your mind. Then comes school, where teachers sincerely do their share in conditioning your mind. Later, it's society in general that continues to condition your mind.

Psychosocial conditioning obviously varies from person to person, depending upon the environment you grow up in.

Attachments

As a baby, you start getting *attached* to your parents who provide you food, comfort and warmth. It works for a few months but then they want time for themselves, too. So they look for some *distraction* for you. They find an answer in "toys." Initially, you're curious about these things that look cute and make funny noises. Slowly, you get *attached* to them. Soon you're hooked on them. "They are mine." The concept of "*mine*" is added to your Acquired Self. With time, the concept of "mine" gets deeper and deeper and the toys get bigger and bigger.

Judging, Reward and Punishment

41

Now your parents go one step further. They start to control your behavior through these toys: If you do what we tell you (*good behavior*), you'll get more toys on your birthday and Christmas, but if you don't do what we tell you (*bad behavior*), then you won't get any toys. Sometimes they even take away your toy to *punish* you for not listening to them. The concept of *good* behavior and *bad* behavior, *reward* and *punishment* is added to your Acquired Self.

Ego

The concept of toys soon gets glorified into the concept of *gifts*. Now you receive toys wrapped up in paper and these are called gifts. The concept of gifts is further refined: you receive a gift because you're *special* and the person who gives you a gift *loves* you. The concepts of "*I am special*" and "*love* through gifts" are added to your Acquired Self.

Excitement and Boredom

Toys, gifts, being special and *being loved* give you momentary *thrill* and *excitement*. However, that soon fades away and you get *bored*. You want more momentary thrill and excitement. You can't wait until your birthday or Christmas. The concept of gifts is so exciting that you can't wait to count the gifts and open them. That's where you get most of your excitement. You may *not* even be interested in what's inside the package. You develop an *insatiable appetite* for momentary thrill and excitement, which only increases as you grow older.

There are a lot of other ways in which your parents provide you with momentary thrill and excitement. Video games are very popular these days. Starting at a very young age, you get your fixes of momentary excitement through these virtual games. Manufacturers of these games fool your parents with sale pitches. "These are great educational tools." "This will improve your kid's dexterity." "After using our game, your kid will be more advanced than other kids in preschool."

Most of these games are built around the concepts of *competition, goal and reward*. You have to achieve certain points, usually by killing some object (troll, demon, spy, etc) called *evil* or *bad*. If you win, you're the good hero and a reward follows. The concepts of *bad, evil, hero, killing, winning and losing* are added to your Acquired Self.

At the same time, you also start getting exposed to stories, books, movies and plays, most of which further deepen the concepts of *good, bad, villain, hero, reward and punishment*. You get strongly attached to these concepts and love to wear T-shirts with pictures of these heroic characters (which cost your parents a whole lot more than a regular shirt!)

Mental Labeling and Judging

These video games, books and movies create mental pictures in your mind, with a story attached as good or bad. That's how the concept of *mental labeling* and *judging* is added to your

Acquired Self. You also hear your parents constantly calling some events and behaviors *good* and others *bad*. They also often use phrases such as "*I like it. I don't like it. I love it, I hate it.*" Soon you start to replicate these phrases.

This *mental labeling and judging* provoke intense emotions inside you in the form of thrill, excitement, sadness, horror and fear. You may have *nightmares* with the random distorted replay of these mental images during your sleep.

ADD (Attention Deficit Disorder)

In some children, this *sensory load* of virtual information from video games, books and movies is so enormous that their developing brain can't handle it. These children start exhibiting signs of sensory overload in the form of *jitteriness*, *disruptive* and *impulsive* behavior and *difficulty focusing*. They become a problem for their teacher, who calls in the parents to have a *session* with the principal of the school.

Upon the teacher's insistence, parents often take their child to a pediatrician who conveniently gives a diagnosis of ADD (Attention Deficit Disorder). The child is then put on a drug to alter the brain chemistry. It's a band-aid approach to calm the kid down so the classroom isn't disrupted. Meanwhile, the root cause for the problem, the Acquired Self, keeps getting bigger and bigger.

Abandonment

Your parents, who are so loving and who you are so attached to, one day decide to leave you with a stranger, called a *baby-sitter*. You feel intense emotional pain of *abandonment*. You cry and cry and cry! Finally, you are distracted by toys or get exhausted from crying and eventually go to sleep.

Later, when your guilt-stricken parents ask the baby-sitter how things went, she lies with a smile on her face and says that you were no problem at all; "I would love to baby sit her again," she says as she receives her hourly wages.

Repeated episodes of this emotionally traumatic experience of abandonment keep adding to your Acquired Self. Please be aware that it's not your parents fault. They are doing what society's Collective Acquired Self has advised them to do. "You should have some private quality time, - just the two of you, away from your children to keep your marriage alive."

Competition and Comparison

Sooner or later, another concept is added to your growing Acquired Self: *comparison* and *competition* which often becomes the main driving force behind your upbringing.

At home, you're compared to your brother, sister, or cousin. You remember your dad saying "Why can't you be like your older brother, John?" Comments like this cause the emotion

45

of *humiliation, worthlessness and jealousy.* All these negative comments with their associated negative emotions get added to your Acquired Self.

You also hear your parents constantly comparing and judging people, events, objects, etc: *"Better than, The best, Worse than, The worst."* All these comparing and judging keeps adding to your Acquired Self. Soon you start replicating them. *"My best friend, My favorite toy, My favorite uncle. My dad is the best in the whole wide world."* Your parents keep reinforcing these ideas into your Acquired Self.

Rules and Consequences

When you enter school, the making of your Acquired Self gets into high gear. Soon you learn you can't be at ease in the morning. Now you need to be at school on time or there will be *consequences* in the form of punishment. You have to follow certain *rules* in your classroom or there will be consequences. You also hear a lot of *rules* at home. Follow them or face the consequences. Initially, you resent these rules and their consequences.

You develop *resentment* against those (parents and teachers) who implement these punishments. Ultimately, you may develop *rebellion against authority.* Ironically, you also develop *fear of authority* as you know they posses the power to punish you.

At school as well as at home, you also learn the concept of how to be good and receive *rewards* in the form of praise, recognition and even some toys. Your parents may start rewarding you with money as an allowance for your good behavior. These rewards give you *excitement*.

The concept of *punishment and reward* keep getting deeper and deeper into your Acquired Self.

Some children are sent to boarding school. Initially you don't like it. You feel the pain of *abandonment*. But soon it gets pushed down by the every day strict reward, punishment drill that is so prevalent in these boarding schools.

More Competition and Comparison

At school, *comparison and competition* is the main driving force. Spelling bee competitions, football games and cheerleader competitions are just a few examples. Kids are also enrolled in dance, gymnastic, skate, music and speech competitions. Plus, there are all the sports competitions: soccer, basketball, volleyball, hockey, swimming and football. Then there are local beauty pageants, debating competitions and academic decathlons. You get the idea.

In teenagers, *competition* for a boyfriend or girlfriend starts to take place. Girls *compare* each other's looks and clothes while boys *compete* to be the captain of the football team. Often there are verbal as well as physical fights. Everyone wants to be *popular, wants to be praised and acknowledged*, wants to *dominate* and *humiliate* the others. The school often becomes a battlefield. Everyone wants to *win* and *defeat* others. The concepts of *victory* and *defeat* get embedded into your Acquired Self. Everyone wants to be a *winner* and not a *loser*. However, in life, you sometimes win and sometimes lose.

Each time you win, you're thrilled and feel superior to others. You receive *praise and validation* from those around you. You feel you're at the top of the world, *in full control*. But these feelings are short-lived and you want more of these exciting feelings.

Wanting More kills *contentment*. You develop a chronic *restlessness*. You're constantly looking for more thrills and excitement. You want to be in charge and in control. When you don't get your fix, you get *frustrated, agitated and bored*.

Each time you lose, you feel *humiliated, inferior, worthless and jealous*; And if you feel that you lost because of unfairness, then you also become *bitter, resentful, hateful, revengeful and angry*.

All of these emotional experiences continue to add to your Acquired Self in the form of *memories*. Over the years, you accumulate tons and tons of memories which become your *emotional baggage*.

More Judging

You are also *judged* constantly at home as well as at school, in the form of your report card, good behavior, bad behavior, good attitude, bad attitude, good manners, bad manners, polite and rude.

Society's Collective Acquired Self gives your personal Acquired Self the concepts of "how everyone should behave." It's as if your Acquired Self is downloaded with a book which describes how everyone in society *should* and *should not* behave.

For example, it tells you *"This is how a true friend should behave... This is how a good boyfriend/girlfriend, husband/wife should behave... This is how a good parent should behave... This is how a good child/student should behave."*

Equipped with this "book of role description," your Acquired Self constantly *judges* others while they judge you.

Expectations

You also build up *expectations* around this "book of role description," naively thinking, "If I do everything by the book, then the other person will keep up his end of the deal." When the other person doesn't behave as expected, you get *disappointed*, *frustrated* and *outraged*.

In addition, you also judge yourself. When you don't or can't behave according to the "software of role description," you criticize yourself. This is the basis of *self-criticism* and *guilt*.

I, Me, My, Mine

The concept of "*I, Me, My, Mine*" continues to embed deeper into your growing Acquired Self. *My friends, my school, my teacher, my books, my home, my neighborhood.* The concept of "I, Me, My, Mine" is the basis of *selfishness* and psychological *separation* from everyone else on the planet.

The Acquired Self Steals your Identity

The concept of "I, Me, My, Mine" creates an *illusion* of who you are. This becomes the axis of your growing Acquired Self. In this way, your Acquired Self hijacks your identity. You lose your true identity and start to believe in this illusory "I" to be who you are.

An innocent, loving, trusting, joyful, contented you is replaced by an agitated monstrous, virtual "I" self who wants to win at all costs. This "I" always *wants more (greed)*, is *self-centered*, *does not trust anyone* and carries a huge load of *worthlessness*, *bitterness*, *jealousy*, *hate* and *anger*. It wants to *defeat*, *control* and also *humiliate* others to take revenge for its own previous humiliating experiences. It is always looking for *momentary thrills*. It is constantly *judging* others while others are *judging* it. Often it is *judging* itself. It looks for *rewards*, *praise* and

50

validation. It easily gets *hurt, frustrated* and *disappointed.*

Now this "monstrous you" enters the so called, real world. *Competition, comparison* and *judging* gets even worse. You see everyone competing for money. Naturally, money becomes your main *goal.* You do it in the name of career and profession. You fight for jobs. Sometimes you win and sometimes you lose. At the workplace, everyone competes for a promotion. Even when you're at the top, you want more: more bonuses, more recognition, more fame. Everyone also remains scared of losing their job, promotion and reputation.

There are no true friends because competition and jealousy kills friendship. You compare yourself to others all the time, just as they compare themselves to you.

Society's collective monster in the form of news and entertainment rigorously conditions you regarding competition and comparison. Just consider how often you hear the words *winner, loser, better than, the best, worse than, the worst, top ten.*

Your Acquired Monster is so competitive that even in social discussions it wants to win the argument. People don't even completely listen to each other. As one monster is making its point, the other is mentally preparing to attack and this goes on back and forth. Two monsters take mental positions and no one can afford to lose the argument.

Everything in life gets focused on winning; and life

51

becomes a battlefield. You see it everywhere - on the freeway, at work, on TV shows. Everyone wants to get ahead. No one wants to lose.

Most men get hooked on sports. By clinging to a team, they are in virtual competition. When your team wins, you get a momentary thrill and when it loses, you feel humiliated and even angry. This cycle continues. You get addicted to it.

Others get addicted to the win-lose cycle of gambling, horse racing, car racing, etc. Sometimes, emotional pains and desire to have momentary thrills are so strong that a person gets addicted to alcohol, drugs or sex.

Many people also get involved in political, social and religious groups and get trapped in the cycle of "win and lose." They experience all the emotions resulting from this game of win-lose. All these experiences keep adding to the growing monstrous Acquired Self.

While competition is usually the main driving force in the making of men's monsters, comparison becomes the driving force for most of women's monsters. They are conditioned by the Society Monster to compare each others looks, clothes, jewelry, etc. They constantly judge others looks as well as their own appearances.

A nice compliment can make you feel on the top of the world: a *momentary thrill*. Then of course, you want more of it.

That means spending more time and money on your appearance.

A negative comment, on the other hand, rips you apart, makes you *sad and sometimes even revengeful*. You get so attached to your looks that even a slight reminder of reality, such as grey hair, a wrinkle or weight gain of a few pounds throws you in a downward spin and creates huge *anxiety*.

The Concept of Romance and Marriage

The Society Monster also downloads the *concept of romance and marriage* into your personal monster, starting from a very young age. All those storybooks and movies about princes and princesses, and later on, TV shows, movies and books about romance feed into your developing Acquired Self.

You also learn about dating games in your early teens. To find a mate, you start competing. In bars and parties, there is intense competition for mates, sometimes resulting in verbal and even physical fights.

As a man, as soon as you can get sex, you have conquered, won the game and you are no longer interested. Now you're on to the next hunt while she chases you. *You are the winner and she is the loser.* You feel high while she feels hurt and low. Your excitement is usually short lived. Sooner or later, you fall in love with a girl and now, she may dump you. *Now she is the winner and you are the loser.*

After playing this game of "win and lose" a few times, people start looking for a serious relationship and marriage. In some cultures, the Society Monster has given the task of searching for a bride or groom to the parents. Now it's the parents who go through intense scrutiny (comparison) while selecting a bride or groom for their son or daughter.

The Honeymoon is Over

After marriage, there is an initial period of excitement which usually wanes in a few months. Then the monster in each one of you starts to act out. *All the piled up anger, humiliation, abandonment, sadness, jealousy and "need to win" starts to surface.* Arguments and fights become routine. Romantic love fades away.

Self Pity

In the meantime, if you also have a child or two, your selfishness is further enhanced. You start to feel that you're working hard for everyone else and have no time for yourself to do the things that you want to do to have fun. Life seems so meaningless and boring.

Working like a Machine

You go to work where everything is routine and stressful: customers, colleagues and bosses are so demanding. You are basically trying to survive all day long. You come home

54

exasperated and tired, often with a headache.

One of you has to get the kids to school, keep house and prepare meals as well. Usually, it's a female, working to be a career woman, raising a family and trying to be a *super mom*.

Morning time is often very stressful because school starts on time. Your monster has learned that there will be consequences if your kid is not on time. Unfortunately, your kid's monster hasn't grasped the whole concept yet. Without being aware, you start yelling at your kids for being late again. Soon, they start to yell back. Now, you're really enraged. "Don't talk to me in that tone, young lady."

Then you have to be at work on time. Most people encounter morning rush hours: bumper to bumper traffic. Scared of the consequences of being late (may lose job), you feel anxious and irritated. You may easily explode in anger if some other driver doesn't behave according to your expectations which arise out of the traffic rules embedded in your Acquired Self.

One of you also has to take your kids to *after-school* and *weekend activities*. You feel obligated to enroll your kids into these activities because those are good for your kids, says the Society Monster. These activities start on time and often you're rushed to make it on time. Often, everyone is yelling at each other and in a bad mood by the time you reach the playground.

If your team loses, the kids feel sad and humiliated and

55

sometime even start crying. As a loving parent, you also endure all these pains. Next time when your team wins, it's the kids and parents on the other side of the field who experience sadness. However, your Monster doesn't let you think about them. It tells you to celebrate your victory and be happy.

At home, you are easily annoyed at the demands of your kids and spouse. Finally, your inner irritation can't take it any more and you yell at them over some little annoyance.

Guilt

Then you feel bad and guilty about it. Why? Because the Society Monster has written a "book of role descriptions." It describes your role as a husband, wife, parent and child and downloads it into your developing Acquired Self at a relatively young age. If you do your role according to the book, Society judges you to be a good husband, wife, father or mother. Otherwise, you are a bad husband, wife or parent. Often, there is a conflict between how you're *supposed* to act according to the software and how you *actually* end up behaving in real life. This is the basis of *guilt*.

Emptiness

You can't even tell anyone how you truly feel about your spouse, children or elderly parent because you're afraid how others will judge you. You feel *isolated* and *lonely*. No one seems to understand you. You are constantly *irritated*. You feel *emptiness* inside you.

Escapes

You look for some relief and often find *escapes* into excessive work, alcohol, sports, drugs, gambling, etc. Many people pursue more and more money. With money, you can buy expensive presents for your spouse, buy a bigger home, buy a more expensive car or take a trip to an expensive vacation resort. From each thing, you get a momentary thrill and excitement, but it fades away fast and returns you to your chronic state of unease, irritation and emptiness.

To pay for these expensive items, you have to work harder. Often you spend most of your time at work, which you don't like, especially if you're a caring parent and want to spend time with your children. This adds to your sense of having *no control over your life* and deepens your frustration. You start hating your job.

On the other hand, some people find relief in being away from their family. It's as if the family is the cause of all of your problems. Often you end up having an *affair*. You find someone who feeds your monster's hunger for praise and validation. Soon, you're in a serious mess. The stress of hiding the affair eventually implodes into a big blow out when your spouse discovers your deceit. Often, it ends in divorce.

Blaming

Now the monster in each of you comes out with full force. It is full of hate, anger and revenge. Each one of you tries to cause as much harm to the other as possible. *Kids are the one in the middle and may suffer the most in the long run.* Each one of you blames the other for all the problems.

Blaming others is one of the features of the Acquired Self. Blaming is actually a form of judging others. It doesn't see any problems in itself, but is quick to find someone else's faults. Your Acquired Self has learned to never admit any faults, because admitting fault means you're a loser. It may also put you at risk for punishment for your actions.

Discipline and Control

You may go through a couple of divorces before you settle down in a long marital relationship, which often requires another role for you - the role of step-parent. Step-parenting creates a host of new emotional challenges, often centered around control issues.

The Society Monster has taught your Personal Monster to treat children in a certain way: "Treat them like a superhero or princess when they are little and as they get older, control their behavior with toys, gifts, money and discipline."

Most parents get frustrated and even quite angry at their

teenagers. On the other hand, teenagers also get very frustrated with their parents to the point that they can't wait to leave the prison of their parent's house. They get tired of hearing "you have to obey my rules while living under my roof."

Teenagers are in the grip of their own monster created by the Society Monster through TV, internet, magazines and video games. Their Monster is taught to disobey, rebel and not follow rules under the illusion of independence and freedom.

Meanwhile, the *Society Monster tells your Monster to discipline your teenagers with rules and the same Society Monster tells teenagers to rebel against the rules.* Interesting, isn't it? The Society Monster plays the trick of *Divide and Conquer.* In this way, it escapes detection and continues to thrive in you and your child. Ironically, neither of you sees the tricks of the Society Monster. Your Monster and your teenager's Monster continue to tangle with each other, leading to frustrations, disappointments and anger.

Loneliness

Then one day, your children leave the house and now you may suffer from what the Society Monster calls the *Empty Nest Syndrome.* What really happened is that you treated your children as possessions and now you don't have that possession and control any more.

Children also serve as a distraction from your own deep

59

seated emotional pains. With them gone, you're faced with the demons stored in your memory box, which is part of your Acquired Self. Children also satisfy your desire to be needed. After their departure, you feel *worthless*.

Now you're middle aged. The Society Monster has already downloaded a bleak picture into your Personal Monster. You're "over the hill" and your looks are fading away. Your children don't need you anymore. You start feeling *worthless and depressed*.

Fear

The Society Monster also forecasts a future in which you lose you health. *Fear* of losing your health is immense. Fear of losing your job, your house and your savings may also settle in.

If your child dates someone you don't approve of, you also develop fear of losing your child.

Anxiety and depression are pretty common at this stage of your life, all created by your own Monster but you don't see it that way. You always blame someone else for your emotional problems.

Hope

Your Society Monster also creates a future for you that it promises will be better than the present and it calls it "*hope*." And it wants you to firmly believe in hope. It often blames most of your stress on your job and promises you *golden years* after retirement. You'll have no responsibilities and can travel and have as much fun as you want.

Bitterness

After your retirement, your dream of golden years is often shaken when you or your spouse is diagnosed with some chronic or incurable illness. You feel cheated. "What did I do to get in this mess and how can I get out of it?" You're a regular visitor to doctors and hospitals. You want your health back, but often the answer is that you *can't.* You get bitter at the system, the government, and even God.

Denial

Now the Society Monster tells you to fight your body dysfunction whether it be cancer, diabetes or heart disease. So you put up a wall of resistance without realizing you are fighting your own body. The Society Monster tells your Monster that you can cheat death. It implies that medical technology can make you live forever. However, when reality hits and someone close to you dies, you become fearful of your own death.

Fear of Poverty, Disability and Death

At this late stage in your life, society considers you a useless, economic burden and even makes numerous jokes about you.

You're probably living on a budget. A great deal of your money is eaten up by the cost of drugs, doctors and hospital bills. You keep *hoping* for a better future as the Society Monster has trained you to do. But you are also *afraid* you may not have enough money left to take care of your needs. You are also afraid of *disability* and *death*. You read stories about nursing homes and get scared. *What if* you end up in a nursing home? You read a horrible story about someone dying a miserable death from cancer, and you become even more fearful. *What if* that happens to me?

It's primarily your Monster who's afraid of dying and wants to live forever. And it continues to suffer from the fear of death. Then one day reality hits and you are gone from this world.

The Acquired Self Continues to Live On!

You are dead, but your Acquired Self has skillfully perpetuated itself through your children. Your children behave and carry on much like your Acquired Self with the special addition of their own Acquired Self. Then, they download all of their Acquired Self into their children and those children repeat it in their children. In this way, the drama of stress created by the Acquired Self goes on forever!

Chapter 7

Instillation of Information

Society's Collective Acquired Self, (what I call the Society Monster), also instills a huge load of information into your developing monstrous Acquired Self.

This is Your Name

Initially it uses your parents (and grandparents) as a tool. They put a carefully selected label on you. They call it your *name*.

This is Your Religion, Culture and Nationality

Parents and grandparents slowly download all sorts of information into you: their religious belief, nationality, customs, traditions, cultural values, eating habits, their likes and dislikes and their personal stories.

You must Acquire More and More Knowledge

The Society monster then uses teachers in school to reinforce information you acquire from your parents. In addition, they download a whole lot more information: the information from storybooks, movies, history books, geography books, science books, etc.

You're encouraged to read and acquire as much information as possible. Your fun and play time starts to decline as you advance through school. Initially, you don't like it. "What happened to all the play and fun I used to have?" However, teachers and parents skillfully use the "reward and punishment" strategy to tame you and often succeed in their mission.

Don't Blame Your Parents or Teachers

Don't blame your parents or teachers for instilling all of this information into your Acquired Self. They do so with good intentions. In their hearts, they believe they're doing you good. They're preparing you to be responsible and productive citizens of the society.

In most cases, your parents also reinforce their cultural and religious ideas by taking you to churches, temples, mosques and celebrating religious and cultural holidays. The idea of nationalism is reinforced by celebrating national holidays.

An Insatiable Appetite for Knowledge

As you grow up, you gain more and more knowledge about the collective human past in the form of history. Your growing Acquired Self keeps gathering all this information and gets bigger and bigger.

By the time you grow up, your monstrous Acquired Self

has an insatiable appetite. It wants to get as much information as possible. It wants to be the *first* one to know the *latest* stories and it doesn't want to miss any *gossip*. So, it starts the day by feeding itself a healthy breakfast by watching TV and reading the newspaper. For the rest of the day, it uses TV, the internet and colleagues as a source for its *food.* It continues to add all sorts of information throughout the day. Then, it makes sure to feed itself a good dinner in the form of the evening news or internet updates. Before going to bed, it uses the 10 o'clock news as a bedtime snack.

Opinions Become Truth

Information in the form of stories, concepts, ideas, beliefs and dogmas becomes an important part of your Acquired Self. Often you don't even realize that most of this information is actually the opinions of others. You start to believe all of this second hand information is the "truth." Then you look at the world through the filters of this acquired information. Consequently, most of your experiences are tainted by those preconceived notions. Hence, you don't have any original experiences!

For example, you look at the appearance of someone and based upon the information in your head, you judge that person without even exchanging a word. This is the basis of *prejudice.*

You may hear about some country. Soon, you regurgitate all the information you have heard about that country including its people, culture and history even though you've never been there and haven't met anyone from that country or culture.

Sometimes two people may even take mental positions and start arguing, each one believing that his information is true and the other person's information is not. This can lead to verbal *violence* and sometimes even physical *violence.*

In the same way, people argue about some figure or event in the collective human past. Everyone believes his information is accurate without realizing that it's simply someone's (the historian's) point of view and obviously these stories are tainted by the historian's own Acquired Self. That's why there are so many conflicting stories about the same *figure* or *event* in the collective human past. Often, one set of stories has been downloaded in the Acquired Selves of people in a group, party or country. Meanwhile, another conflicting set of stories is downloaded into the Acquired Selves of another group, party or country. Collectively, people in each group believe their story to be true because they identify with their group of people and they also see everyone around them believing the same story.

Often these stories perpetuate *hate, grievances and revenge* and sometimes can lead to verbal or physical *violence* and even battles and wars.

Chapter 8

Creation of the Past and Future

"Past and future" are major components of the Acquired Self. Have you ever wondered what really *is* the past and future? Use logic and you will realize that whatever happened in the past is not happening right now. Whatever may happen in the future, of course, is not happening right now. The past is dead and gone and the future never arrives. Hence, both are virtual and unreal, aren't they?

Just like a monster, the past and future are *virtual*, and each has huge power over your Acquired Self. It may seem they are real, but in fact they are not. Can you show me your past or future, in reality, right now, not as a mental abstraction? Of course not! We cannot see, hear, touch, smell or taste our past or future.

The past was real when it happened, but it is not happening right now. Hence, it is unreal at the present moment. The future never happens. When it happens, it happens in the present moment. The past and future are nothing but mental abstractions. Both are created by the mind.

How your Mind Creates Your Past and Future

For a while, I used to ponder the question: How does the

mind creates the past and future? Then one day, the answer just struck me, when I wasn't even thinking about it. I was sitting in my backyard looking at the sky, clouds, birds, flowers, trees and feeling the breeze. Then a friend of mine visited me. We had a chat for about 15-20 minutes and then he left. About five minutes after he left, I had a flashback of my friend's visit. *I heard him calling my name, then coming and sitting on the chair next to mine. I could recall his conversation and eventual departure.* The whole event was as fresh in my mind as if it was happening right now.

A realization happened that truly transformed me. I realized that my friend's visit was an event, with a beginning and an ending. However, my mind took a mental picture of it, attached the whole conversation as a story and labeled it as a good experience. This triggered a feeling of happiness and the entire bundle of *picture, story, mental labeling* and *provoked emotion* was stored as a sweet memory. Now my mind can go back to it any time it wants and experience the whole event over and over again. That's how the event is kept alive, although in reality, the event has ended.

Events happen all the time. *Each event has a beginning and an ending.* But our mind takes a mental picture of the whole event, attaches a story to go with it, labels it good or bad, which triggers a good or bad emotion, and the entire bundle is then placed in the memory box. There it stays alive, although in reality, it is dead and gone.

68

The mind continues to add mental pictures of events, with attached stories and triggered emotions, and places them in the memory box and that's how it creates the so called *past*.

With this background, your mind also tries to figure out how the next event is going to be (or rather how it should or should not be); At times, it even creates a virtual picture. Each thought provokes an emotion and the whole complex of self-generated thoughts and emotions, it calls the *future*.

The Busy Mind

The "past and future" is all in our heads, isn't it? It's all virtual... an unreal, mental abstraction... an illusion. In reality, neither the past nor the future exists. *However, to the mind they are real.* Why? Because the mind creates them. How could it not believe in its own creation?

Since the mind creates these entities called the past and the future, it loves to dwell in them. You could call them its home. That's why your mind stays in the so called past and future.

Medically speaking, the more often this network of memory neurons (brain cells) is traveled, the stronger the network of neurons becomes. Then impulses can run more easily, without much impedance, through these neuronal networks. This is the basis of the *busy mind,* which runs through the same old events, thoughts and emotions of the so called past, as well as projected thoughts and emotions it calls the future.

69

Stress Created by the "Past and Future"

By keeping the old dead events alive, your busy mind keeps the fire of old emotions burning inside you. It calls them "my past" and "my memories." It judges these memories as either good or bad.

By replaying bad memories, your busy mind continues to experience the negative emotions attached to these memories in the form of *humiliation, anger, hate, bitterness, jealousy and revenge.* Subsequently, your body also gets affected by these negative emotions.

By replaying good memories, your busy mind starts to *miss* those wonderful experiences and becomes *sad.* Subsequently, your entire body feels the impact of this sadness as well.

The Mind Wants to Change Its Past

Here's another interesting phenomenon. The busy mind wants to control the virtual world of memories. It is strongly attached to sweet memories, but it wants to run away from bad memories Therefore, it tries to modify the stories and events.

For example:
"If I'd only skipped work that day. I never would have had that accident. Now, instead I'm disabled forever."

"If my teacher hadn't humiliated me in front of entire class, I'd be a happy person today."

"Why didn't I see the clues? He's been cheating on me all along! Why did I marry him?"

"Why did I take this job? My boss is so stingy and demanding."

"Why didn't I sell my stocks six months ago when the financial market was so high?"

But of course, the busy mind can't change what has already happened. It feels *annoyed, frustrated, angry* and sometimes *guilty* as well. The more it tries to change those painful memories, the stronger they get. As I mentioned earlier, those networks of brain cells which are traveled more, grow stronger. It is an irony, but the busy mind doesn't know it.

The Mind wants to Secure a Happy Future

In addition, the busy mind doesn't want any bad event to happen again, ever! It wants perfect *security*. The Society Monster trains your individual Monster to learn from the past. Therefore, it wants to create a perfect world for itself in which there are only good things and bad things do not exist. It wants to create a paradise for itself. Therefore, it continues to generate new thoughts along the lines of how to prevent bad events from

71

happening again.

The "What If" Syndrome

But then another thought erupts: "*What if I can't prevent it from happening again?*" That triggers huge *fear and anxiety*.

Caught up in the "What if, What may, What will I do Syndrome," the busy mind creates a virtual movie and in this way, creates perpetual *fear* in you. In the pursuit of security and peace, your busy mind robs you of any peace of mind and torments you with everlasting fear. How counterproductive!

Some examples:

"*What if I get stung by the bee again?!*"

"*What if my audience makes fun of me again?*"

"*What if I lose it again?*"

"*What if I become poor again?*"

"*What if I lose my friends again?*"

"*What if I lose my job again?*"

"*What if I get dumped again?*"

"What if I'm late again?"

"What if I miss my flight again?"

"What if no one pays attention to me again?"

"What if my wife cheats again?"

"What if my boss insults me again?"

"What if I become fat again?"

"What if I have an attack of asthma again?"

The Society Monster reinforces this syndrome of "What if, What may, What will I do" in the form of information conveyed by newspapers, books, TV and the internet. It teaches you to learn from the past. Meanwhile, the busy mind inside you, your Monster, keeps generating huge amounts of *fear and anxiety*.

The "What's Next" Mindset

Observe your busy mind and you will see it always stays in the "what's next" mode. In this way, it always rushes to the next moment. When the so called next moment arrives, it is the present moment, isn't it? In this way, "the next moment" exists only in your head. It is virtual, a phantom, an illusion.

What is <u>real</u> is always the present moment. By rushing to the next moment, your conditioned mind skillfully keeps avoiding what's real - the present moment. Amazing!

How does the mind become so dysfunctional? Use logic and you realize it is the conditioning of the mind that makes it so dysfunctional. The conditioning starts in early childhood and never ends. Look around and see how society conditions everyone's mind to *run* to the next moment. Some examples include next day (which it calls tomorrow), next month, next year, next birthday, next class, next school, next holiday, next appointment and next promotion.

Staying in "what's next" mode, the mind does not experience "what's now" and creates a constant agitated state inside you in the form of "rushed feeling." You see it everywhere. Even on the freeways, everyone is rushing to the next moment, which often results in accidents. Waiting in line at the post office, airport and grocery store, everyone feels agitated, because they're in the mindset of "what's next." If there is a *delay* for one reason or another, the mind in the "what's next" mode gets more agitated and creates more stress for itself and others.

The Unconscious and Subconscious Mind

The emotional experiences from very early childhood cannot be remembered. In traditional psychology, we call this the *Unconscious Mind*. The emotional experiences from later childhood and adult life, ordinarily remain under the surface of consciousness, but can be easily recalled. In traditional

74

psychology, this is called the *Subconscious Mind.* Both the Unconscious and Subconscious minds are part of the Acquired Self. Emotions buried in the Acquired Self at the Unconscious and Subconscious level continue to stay alive and tremendously affect our psychological state.

The Expansion of Past and Future

In addition to personal experiences, the busy mind also borrows experiences of others and considers them its own. For example, you watch a story on TV about someone who died a miserable death from cancer, leaving behind young children who struggled to adjust. Your mind snapshots the images conveniently shown on TV, attaches the provided story, judges it to be bad (which triggers sad emotions) and the entire bundle gets stored in your memory box. The mind then generates another thought: "This must never happen to me!" Then another thought pops up: "But what if...? " Before you know it, you' re having an anxiety attack.

Now imagine how often you read stories in books, magazines and newspapers. Add to that the stories you watch on TV, the internet and movie screens. Obviously, these are the experiences of people you've never even met. Some stories happened thousands of miles away or many centuries ago. Many are not even real experiences, but simple fiction. However, your busy mind clings to those experiences of others (real or fictional) as if they are your own experiences. Now, can you imagine the

75

size of your memory box? That's why you have such a busy mind. The busy mind is your Monster.

Collective Human Past and Future

Your Society Monster, which is basically a reflection of your Monster, also creates its own virtual past and a virtual future. It likes to dwell in its past which is calls *history*. It also promises you a future in which everything is good and nothing bad ever happens. It promises you ultimate security.

But then it also gives you "What if, What may, and What will we do" Syndrome. It wants you to never forget its past and thus, continues to propagate *hate, grievances and revenge*. It also spreads *fear and anxiety* about the so called tomorrow. It creates hypothetical fearful situations for you, and then tells you how to prepare to deal with the frightening situations as if they were happening right now. In doing so, it continues to torment you. This is one way the Society Monster keeps you under its control.

Chapter 9

Virtual Present

In addition to past and future, your Acquired Self also creates a *virtual* present. To the Acquired Self, its present is *not virtual* but *real*. Why? Because your Acquired Self creates it. Obviously, it believes its own creation to be true. Moreover, everyone around you believes in their virtual present. So does your Acquired Self. For these reasons, you don't ever question the virtual nature of your present. Instead, you believe it to be true.

What is Virtual Present?

Your virtual present mainly consists of a number of concepts, relationships and possessions. For example, My family, My friends, My job/profession, My house, My pets, My car, My neighbor, My political party, My religious organization, My club, My sports team, My health, My looks, etc.

How Your Virtual Present Creates Stress for You

Your mind judges your conceptual present to be good or bad. For example, if you don't have a job, friends, boyfriend/girlfriend, spouse, children, house, desired weight, desired looks, etc., you will feel quite *miserable*. Often, there is an underlying sense of *failure* as the Society Monster has drilled down the concept of success and failure into your Acquired Self.

Even when you have everything going for you; a well paying job/profession, family and friends, house, good looks, etc, you will experience stress from underlying *fear of losing* these possessions, relationships or achievements. In addition, relationships always create some *irritation, annoyance, jealousy, anger, guilt, sadness or dissatisfaction*. These could be your relationships at home, at work, with friends, with neighbors, at a social club, at political or religious organizations, etc.

Therefore, you experience stress whether your "present life" is a success or a failure. Amazing, isn't it?!

So What is the Real Present?

The Real Present is what you *see, hear, smell, taste* and *touch*. We have five senses that create reality for us. So the real present is what you sense with one of your senses and NOT what is in your head.

Chapter 10

Escapes

When you're stressed out and can't take it any more, you reach out for help: any way to get rid of your stress. And who comes to your rescue? The very architect of your stress, the Society Monster, disguised as your friend.

Your Society Monster, the Collective Acquired Self of society, conveniently provides you with a long list of "solutions to stress." Your Monster graciously embraces all of these ideas and hopes to get rid of all stress in your life. However, these ideas only work temporarily at the most. Soon, you're back to your usual state of stress. In this way, these solutions are merely temporary escapes from stress.

Some examples of escapes:

Vacations

In general, when you're stressed out, you're advised to take a break, chill out, go on vacation. But what function does a vacation serve? It temporarily removes you from your stressful environment, right? You get relief from the outer stress. However, if you observe carefully, you'll see that even on vacation, you carry your busy mind, your Acquired Self, with you. Soon, your Acquired Self starts to create stress even though you're on vacation to relax. You may find yourself easily irritated if things don't go your way. You start judging, complaining and blaming others. You create a load of stress for yourself and others.

Imagine someone sitting on the beach, supposedly relaxing for their well-earned vacation, but actually telling horrible stories they've heard about. "Did you watch, see, hear ...." is how it usually starts and then everyone jumps in with their own stories. They all try to outdo each other with more compelling, more dramatic and more appealing stories.

While sitting in a five star hotel lobby in Hawaii, this busy mind gyrates with Wall Street's going up and down. Another one watches football, while his emotions soar up and plummet down as his team's score fluctuates. Another person watches 24 hour news to catch up with all the bad news that happened in the last 24 hours. Mustn't miss any of the destructive chaos of the world.

For some people, every day becomes a mission even when they are on vacation. They could be walking through a forest, but they'll have a map firmly clamped in hand. "Two hundred yards ahead, we should be at the Sherman Tree. We'll take two photos and then we'll continue south on the trail for a quarter mile until we reach the Tracker's Hut."

On your vacation, you may find some moments of peace, but observe what you have to do to experience those peaceful moments. You have to shut off your cell phone. Sit on the beach by yourself, watch that beautiful sunset or walk among the trees, observing all the serenity of the forest. Unfortunately, these moments are usually short lived.

Remember your last Hawaiian (fill in your favorite spot) vacation? You watched a beautiful sunset. For a moment, you were in awe... Speechless and mesmerized... but seconds later, you were back to your usual habit of comparing: "This sunset is more dramatic (or less dramatic) than the one I saw in Florida (or where-ever) last year." Then you might be reminded of all the *bad* things that happened on that trip. Pretty soon your mind completely wanders off in that direction, now completely oblivious to that awesome sunset.

For a majority of the time, people stay in the grip of their busy mind no matter where they are. Vacations are no exception. Therefore, when you come back from your vacation, you're so tired and exhausted, you need another vacation to unwind from this vacation.

Thrill and Excitement

Another way to escape the stress of daily living is to seek out thrills and excitement. Young people in particular are more likely to seek out thrill and excitement. *But it's never enough.* As soon as the excitement fades, they're bored again. They want more excitement.

81

The cycle of boredom and excitement continues and can lead to addictions such as gambling, partying, alcohol, drugs, irresponsible sexual behavior, etc.

Entertainment

Another way to run away from stress is to get entertained by TV, movies, internet, books, magazines and newspapers. With few exceptions, almost everyone is addicted to these activities. By engaging in these activities, you temporarily forget about stressful situations, such as your job or illness of your loved one, which is your outer stress. However, your inner stress stays with you.

For example, you may find yourself disagreeing with the opinions expressed in a movie, getting upset with some guest on a talk show, feeling sorry for the singer who deserved to win a certain prestigious award but didn't, or getting furious at the referee of a basketball game whose unfairness led to the defeat of your team or feeling sad at the sufferings of a character in the book or a movie.

Of course, at some point, you have to leave the TV or internet and face your stressful situation again. Meanwhile, you can't wait to leave the stressful situation and to go back to TV, internet or book (or whatever other entertainment you choose).

Hope

What is hope? Look at it deeply with logic. You realize that hope is actually running away from your present stressful situation and finding an escape into a future that you wish to be better. You're dissatisfied with your virtual present moment and hope the future will be better.

There are three components to what we call Hope:

1. Your mind, your Acquired Self, is dissatisfied with the present situation.
2. It creates a virtual future
3. It wishes to control this virtual future in order to feel secure and happy.

Your Acquired Self learns this pattern of dealing with stressful situations from the Society Monster. Everyone so deeply believes in *hope* that it is almost impossible for people to take a deep, logical look at it. There is some kind of sacredness and heroism attached to the concept of "Hope." Therefore, "Hope" is a wonderful escape because the Society Collective Acquired Self strongly encourages you to be trapped in it.

Positive Thinking

Society has coined another wonderful escape for you: positive thinking! How often you have heard about it and tried it? It may work for a while. However, it doesn't get rid of your inner stress. Sooner or later, you're back to your usual state of stressful living.

What is positive thinking? Let's examine it by using logic. You try to replace your *negative* thoughts with *positive* thoughts. What you are actually trying to accomplish is to change the *composition of your Acquired Self*, that's all. However, you are still in the grip of your Acquired Self, the source of all of your inner stress. That's why *positive thinking* is an escape from your inner stress, but not a cure!

Medications

Sooner or later, these usual escapes don't work any more. You stay agitated, irritated, angry, lonely, bored, sad, fearful, anxious and/or depressed.

The Society Monster has created another great escape: prescription drugs. These are used to stabilize your mood and to treat your attention deficit, anxiety and depression. To justify the use of these drugs, you're told that you have "chemical changes" in your brain and you need these medications to fix those chemical changes.

But how did you develop these chemical changes? No one asks this question. No one is born with these chemical changes because newborns don't have these psychological problems. These medicines keep a lid on your inner stress as long as you take them. Most people relapse if they go off these medicines. Many people need to increase the dose or add more medicines to push down the painful emotions arising out of inner stress.

Getting to the Root of Escapes

Using logic, if you look at this whole drama of escapes, it's apparent that you're running away from "what is." That's why all these activities are actually escapes, hide outs ... And who teaches you all of these escapes? It's society, isn't it?

In other words, the Society Monster, working through your Acquired Monster, creates all the stress for you in the first place. *And when you cannot tolerate this stress anymore and there is a chance you may look deeper and figure out who really is at the root of your stress, the Society Monster distracts your attention and lures you away with a lot of escapes. In this way, the Society Monster and your Personal Monster escape detection by you and continue to thrive. Devious, isn't it?* As I said earlier, your Monster is very treacherous.

The important question you have to ask yourself is this: Is it possible to live a life where you don't need to escape from your stress, but rather live a stress-free life and when stress arises, you face it, instead of running away from it?

In the remainder of this book, I describe a **3-step** approach to get rid of stress from its roots and live a stress-free life. That's what a true stress cure is.

Step 1

Freedom from the Acquired Self

Chapter 11

Freedom from the Acquired Self

Now you understand the root cause of your stress actually resides inside you, your Acquired Self. On the surface, stress seems to be due to *this or that*. In fact, it is your conditioned mind, your Acquired Self, that reacts to *this or that* and creates stress.

The source of stress lies inside you. Therefore, the solution must also reside inside you. You don't depend on any outward source to free you from stress. Don't you feel empowered?

You can be free of stress by freeing yourself from your Acquired Self. Only you can do it. Freed from the Acquired Self, you're in touch with your True Self, the source of true happiness, joy, love and peace. Your True Self is the place where no stress ever exists!

We can express this observation in a mathematical equation:

Total self = True self + Acquired self
True self = Total self − Acquired self

Freedom from the Acquired Self equals freedom from stress.

How to be Free of the Acquired Self

In order to be free of your Acquired Self, you have to separate yourself from it. Only then you can see it for what it is. However, as long as you identify with your Acquired Self, you can never see its true colors. As long as you and your Acquired Self are stuck together, obviously you can never be free of it.

When you're in the grip of your Acquired Self, you immediately react to what others say or do. These automatic reactions often cause more stress for you. Later on, when you come to your senses, you often regret what you said or did.

<u>Don't react immediately!</u>

You need to stop your Acquired Self from automatically taking control of your actions and emotions. Take a *pause* before you react to someone's comment or action.

During this pause, start counting your breath, while at the same time, feel the rage, the fear, the hate or whatever emotion there is. However, fully realize that it is your Acquired Self (and not the true you) who is angry, hateful or fearful. Don't get consumed by the emotion. Be aware of the *present moment*, the *space* inside you in which this whole drama is taking place. The *True You is in essence that space, the present moment.*

While fully aware of the space, feel and watch the drama your Acquired Self creates. Don't run away from it. After a little while, your Monster (Acquired Self) will calm down.

Use Logic

Now use *logic*, the most wonderful tool we humans have. Why? Because the Acquired Self is always *illogical* and can't stand the blazing sunshine of logic. Therefore, use logic and see the true colors of your Acquired Self. See for yourself who is really at the root of all of the stress.

What is logic? When I use the word logic, I mean simple logic, the common sense that we all humans are born with. We don't need to go to school to learn it. Don't confuse it with "rationalization" that people often use to justify their actions. Rationalization, intellectualization, reasoning and justification stem out of the Acquired Self.

In order to use your true, simple logic, you have to be free from any conditioning. Otherwise, it will be tainted by your conditioned mind: all the concepts, opinions, ideas, beliefs, knowledge and previous experiences swirling in your mind, which is your Acquired Self, the Monster within you.

When you use simple logic you clearly see your Acquired Self as the *mastermind* of all of your stress. In the next several chapters, we will look at various layers of the Acquired Self and how to be free of them.

89

In Everyday Living, See your Acquired Self in Action

Everyday living gives you the best opportunity to observe your Acquired Self, the Monster within. So, be aware of your Monster in your everyday life. See it rising, trying to take control of you and influencing your thoughts, emotions and actions. Once you see it clearly and you know it's not your true self, the Monster starts losing its power over you.

That's how you get freedom from your Monster. *You don't fight it, hate it or run away from it. That will only strengthen it. Simply seeing it for what it is will liberate you from its tight grip.*

Examples:

You are just about to point out to your wife one more time that she needs to lose weight. Stop for a moment. Use logic and you'll see that it's actually your Monster at play: the Monster of fear that she'll lose her health/looks and the Monster of control who wants to control her behavior.

Your wife's Monster takes your advice as criticism, insult or attack. In addition, her Monster expected love, not criticism from her loving husband. So it gets hurt, and responds to your Monster by defending itself: It puts up a wall of resistance and may fight back with an equally insulting remark. Only when you fully realize the whole interaction is between two Monsters, will you stop commenting about her weight. You'll be amazed how

90

nicely she starts to respond to you.

When you are just about to complain to your husband that he's always glued to the TV watching sports, take a pause and realize that it's your Monster trying to control your husband's behavior.

When you are about to yell at your kid for not listening to you, pause and observe your Monster. Once you clearly realize that it's your Monster trying to control your kid's behavior, you will stop yelling at your kid. Only then you can sit down and communicate with your kid with love and kindness. You will be amazed at the results.

Next time when you get upset or bored, and start walking towards the refrigerator to pull out that carton of ice-cream, stop for a moment. Use logic and you'll clearly see that you are not hungry at all. So why eat? Then you will be able to see that it is your Monster luring you and providing you with the escape, and actually sabotaging your health. Obviously you say No to this Monster and get out of the prison of stress-eating.

Next time you see your anger rising inside you because of your kids, parents, friends, employees, customers, bosses, etc., pause for a moment and see clearly that it's your Monster who is upset and outraged and wants to act through you. Only then you can say No to your Monster and not act out in the way it wants you to. Then you can analyze the situation in a logical manner and take necessary steps to accomplish whatever needs

91

to be done.

You are in your sixties and doing fine. Then one day, you read in the newspaper that someone important died of a cancer. Your Monster triggers a thought… What if I have cancer? This creates another thought of possibly losing your health, autonomy and ultimately dying. This creates a huge amount of fear. You start feeling your heart pounding. You feel uneasiness and anxiety. Then you start wondering who'll take care of your wife if you die, which further worsens your fear and suddenly, you've got a full fledged panic attack.

Even in the midst of this panic attack, pause, take some deep breaths, and start counting your breaths. Look around and see what is actually happening in front of you. Feel the space inside your chest. At the same time, feel the fear but don't get consumed by it. Fully realize that it is your Monster who is fearful. Your True Self, space, is untouchable. Then use logic. Ask yourself: Do I have cancer at this moment? Am I losing my autonomy at this moment? You realize you really don't have any problems at this moment. Then you also clearly see that it is actually your Monster playing tricks with you by creating an imaginary future. The moment you clearly see the Monster for what it is, an entity separate from you, it starts to lose its power over you. Using logic, you also tell your mind: "I will deal with any medical condition, if and when it arises." Make a mental note to discuss it with your doctor on your next visit. *Stress completely evaporates and you move on with your everyday life.*

92

Don't Create any More Stress for Yourself or Others

When we act under the influence of our Monster, we don't think clearly. Our actions are often illogical, which creates more problems instead of solving them. On the other hand, once we are free of our Acquired Self, we can truly think logically and take necessary actions. These actions are more effective and don't create stress for yourself or others.

For example, if someone insults you, you immediately fight back by insulting that person. Often the other person fights back and then you fight back, too. Before you know it, this verbal fight escalates into a physical fight. Some people don't fight back verbally or physically at that moment, but continue to harbor bitterness against that person and seek opportunities to take revenge. In either case scenario, you create a lot of stress for yourself and the other person.

On the other hand, once you have already gained the wisdom of not reacting immediately to peoples' remarks, you will pause for a moment. You will feel the anger rising inside you. You will also clearly see that it's not the true you, but your monster self who is outraged. With a little more logic, you also see the one who is insulting you is actually doing so under the influence of his/her Monster. Then you don't hold any bitterness, grudge or hate towards that person.

Once your Monster has calmed down, you may say something or take some action which will be a whole lot more effective and will not create stress for yourself or the other person.

Don't be Frustrated if You are Unable to See Your Acquired Self

Sometimes you may not be able to take a *pause* and before you know it, you have said or done something under the influence of your Acquired Self. After a while, you'll realize what actually happened and be able to take a logical look at the whole incident. And that's okay. It takes practice to change your life-long conditioned patterns, but as long as you can see these reactions as a function of your Acquired Self, you are getting freedom from your Monster.

For example, someone cuts you off on the freeway. You feel enraged and as a knee jerk reflex, you honk at him or give him the finger. Once your rage settles down, if you can see with logic what really happened, you can be completely transformed. Let's examine this whole drama with logic. It's your Monster and the other driver's Monster in full action, isn't it? His Monster wants to win, get ahead and is thrilled at victory. Your Monster on the other hand, feels like a loser and tries to fight back.

Once you can clearly see your Monster, the next time you will relax and laugh at your own Monster. Instead of fighting back, you'll continue to drive on safely. Stress will not even touch you.

Stay Alert and Vigilant

Often, your Acquired Self will try to trick you back into your old habitual thinking and reactions. Therefore, it is important to stay alert and vigilant. Keep seeing your Acquired Monstrous Self in action with vigilant eyes. You may even be amused or break into laughter when you observe how ridiculous and persistent your Monster is... how it wants you to believe in something that is not happening at all in reality. The moment you can see your Acquired Self as an acquired entity, but not who you really are, it starts to lose its power over you. With this realization, you'll observe your thoughts fading away. Often you will need to see your Monster many times before you are finally free of it.

Do Not Underestimate the Power of your Acquired Self

Do not underestimate the power of your Monster. It has strong roots and will do all it can to continue to control your thoughts and actions. After all, it consists of your life-long mental habits, ideas, traditions and belief system, all of which were bestowed upon you by your loving parents and society. It also consists of your own experiences which in addition to psychological pain, also holds loving memories.

"How can I get rid of all of this?" your Acquired Self says and puts up emotional resistance. "After all, everyone else is like me so this must be my true nature." Your Monster tries to convince you and may even succeed temporarily.

However, if you're determined and pay attention to this Monster rising inside you, you'll be amazed how it starts losing power over you. You'll observe your Monster in constant competition and comparison with other monsters. Your Monster wants to control the behavior of others and gets very upset if not obeyed. Other monsters behave in much the same way. They fight back and want to control your monster instead. A war between monsters is happening all the time. Everyone wants to be the winner! No one wants to be the loser!

It is relatively easy to see the so called negative components of the Acquired Self such as competition, comparison, judging, bad memories, what if syndrome, etc. But it is much more difficult to see the so called good components of the Acquired Self such as good memories, noble ideas, heroic missions, etc.

To be free of the Acquired Self, you need to see it in all of its colors, shapes and forms.

Compassion Automatically Arises

Except for a few enlightened persons, the vast majority of humans are hijacked by their monster minds. It's like a mental illness afflicting mankind. How can you be angry with mentally sick people? You can only feel compassion for them and try to awaken them from their sickness of ignorance. This realization will completely transform you.

But be careful. Your Acquired Self can easily sneak back in wearing new clothes so to speak and tell you to go on a noble mission to awaken other people.

Remember, your responsibility is to be free of your *own* Acquired Self and that's all! However, if someone asks you for advice or guidance, you can share information, but stay vigilant and alert so that your Acquired Self does not creep back in the form of *ego*.

Transformation Automatically Takes Place

Once you realize that you are separate from your Acquired Self, a process of transformation begins. Then your every day life gives you plenty of opportunity to see your Acquired Self in action. Each time you see it as an entity separate from the True you, it loses its power over you. Then, instead of being upset with some one, you will be grateful to him that his so called bad remark or behavior provided you with the opportunity to see your own Acquired Self and be free of it. In other words, hostility will be automatically replaced by gratefulness.

Caution: Simply feel this gratefulness inside you. Do not express it to the other person because it will only strengthen his Acquired Self.

In Summary

In order to find a true solution, you have to look at the

97

problem itself and not run away from it. Only then is there a real chance of getting to the root of the problem and getting rid of it forever. To look at the problem, you must use *logic,* the most powerful tool available to human beings.

Your Acquired Self is at the root of your psychological problems. Freedom from the Acquired Self equals freedom from stress. In order to be free of your Acquired Self, the *Monster* within, you need to be *aware* of the Monster. You can be free of the Acquired Self by taking the following steps:

1. Pause and don't react immediately.
2. See the Acquired Self in action. Feel the *emotions* it creates, but also be fully aware of the present moment, the *space* in which all of this drama takes place. Be the *observer.*
3. Use logic and realize you are not the Acquired Self. You are separate from the Acquired Self. This is the most critical point.
4. Stay aware and vigilant.
5. Don't get frustrated if you sometimes fail.
6. See the Acquired Self in all of its colors, shapes and forms.

In the next several chapters, let's use the sharp knife of logic and dissect through the multiple layers of the Acquired Self.

Chapter 12

Selfishness

Almost everyone is selfish in one way or another. People often don't see selfishness in themselves, but readily note it in others. If you want to be free of selfishness, instead of running away from it, you need to look at it with logic. Only then, you may find the answer.

The Root Cause of Selfishness

Using logic, let's explore what is at the root of selfishness. Why is someone selfish? A selfish person totally identifies with his *Acquired Self*. In fact, it is the total identification with the Acquired Self that makes a person selfish.

When you're totally in the grip of your Acquired Self, you're operating from what we can call, "I, My, Me, Mine" Syndrome.

I, My, Me, Mine Syndrome

As we observed earlier in the book, the concept of " I, My, Me, Mine" is added to your Acquired Self at a very early age: *My toys, My dog, My room, My school, I am a princess, I am Superman....* This concept is at the center of your Acquired Self.

You could call it the *axis of your Monster.* You identify with this "I, My, Me, Mine" and seriously believe that's who you are. It steals your identity and creates tons of stress for you as well as those around you.

This concept of "I, My, Me, Mine" continues to expand as you grow up. The Society Monster feeds this concept to you as a sugar coated pill it calls "individuality." As a young person, you start to believe in *My school, My friends, My enemies, My basketball team, My girlfriend/boyfriend, My pet, I am beautiful, I am ugly, I am a winner, I am a loser.*

As a middle age person, you often add *My career, My house, My family, My neighborhood, My town, My country, My political party, My religion, My culture, I am rich, I am poor, I own an expensive car.*

As an older person, you might add *My knowledge, My wisdom, My prestige, My past. I have diabetes, I am fighting cancer, I am old.*

This concept of "I, My, Me, Mine" separates you from the rest of world and is the basis of selfishness. When you're in the grip of "I, My, Me, Mine," you work for your own interests. Nothing is more important than to take care of Me and My interests. Whenever you're dealing with other people, you ask "What's in it for Me?" Isn't that what selfishness is?

True Freedom from Selfishness

What is this "I, My, Me, Mine?" If you use logic, you realize that it's simply a concept, an idea, an illusion and nothing more. It's a phantom! Simply a collection of thoughts.

The moment you realize the true illusory nature of this "I, My, Me, Mine," you are free from it. Then you see things clearly, as they really are:

- A car, not My car
- A house, not My house
- A means to make a living, not My career.
- A human being, not My friend, My enemy, My wife or My husband, My employee or My boss.
- An animal, not My pet.

You get the idea!

With this realization, an incredible freedom from selfishness flows in you. When you're free from "I, Me, My, Mine," you're free from selfishness. For example, you realize that your wife is actually a human being, no different from you. She has the same basic needs as you. You don't need to have a separate bank account for yourself.

You see your employee as another human being just like you, no different. You don't need to keep all the profits for yourself and lie to your employees that your company is losing money.

Once free from "I, Me, My, Mine," you can truly help someone else, without always thinking "what's in it for Me." Only then you can be free of your selfish motives. When there is no "I, Me, My, Mine," you don't work for "My interests." This is the end of selfishness!

"We, Us, Our" Syndrome

Often people get attached to a certain social, political or religious idea which then becomes the center of a collective "We, Us, Our" syndrome, which is simply an extension of "I, My, Mine." It creates a clannish mentality. People may work together for their collective interests and may think they are not selfish. However, look deeper and realize that now you're working for the interests of your own "Clan." You are *still* in the grip of selfishness.

Chapter 13

Loneliness

Most people can't stand loneliness. They feel bored, restless and agitated. They compulsively look for activities to stay busy. People run away from loneliness and find refuge in socializing, partying, talking on the telephone or staying connected through the internet.

Being lonely implies you don't have any friends, that you're a failure. Many also feel sorry for themselves. Some even get depressed.

Is it possible to be free of loneliness without running away from it? Use logic. If you want to be free of loneliness, first you have to fully understand it.

Why are you lonely? You will probably answer "'because I am alone." In fact, what you actually imply is that someone who had become part of you, is not with "you" any more. Isn't that the truth? If you look deeper, you realize that the root of loneliness is "I, Me, My, Mine" syndrome. For example, "I'm lonely because *My* husband is not with *Me*." "I'm lonely because *My* wife passed away."

Many people suffer from loneliness, although they may

103

have a large circle of family and friends. When you're in the grip of "I, My, Me, Mine," you create a psychological wall between yourself and everyone else. Then you live in a tiny bubble of your own and look at everyone else through it. You obviously feel isolated and lonely but have no clue why you feel this way. You may hear your inner voice complaining, *"no one understands me."* However, you don't understand why no one understands you. Then another voice chimes in. "Loneliness is not a good thing. It's a sign of failure. I must get rid of my loneliness." Then you find a way to run away from loneliness. The usual escapes include joining a social, political or religious organization, partying, chit-chatting and texting.

The Root Cause of Loneliness

If you want to be free of loneliness, you have to take a deeper look at loneliness instead of running away from it. Psychologically speaking, when you are enslaved by "I, My, Me, Mine," you're separated from every other human being on the planet and of course, you are lonely.

True Freedom from Loneliness

If you want to be free of loneliness, you need to be free of "I, My, Me, Mine." Only then will you start to see the things the way they actually are:

- A human being, not My husband
- A human being, not My friend or My enemy

104

Then you realize the next person in the street is another human being, not your friend or your enemy. You sense an inner connectedness to every living being on the planet. Loneliness simply evaporates! You don't have to employ certain techniques to get rid of loneliness as the Society Monster teaches you to do, such as "get involved in social activities." The simple realization that "you are not who you thought you were" will liberate you from the prison of loneliness. The simple dissociation from "I, My, Me, Mine" Syndrome, will free you from loneliness.

Q: Some enlightened people live alone. Isn't that loneliness?

A: When a person is truly enlightened, which simply means completely free of the Acquired Self, they may sit alone, but are not bored or unhappy. They enjoy the solitude - the joy of being. They are free from "I, My, Me, Mine" Syndrome. They are not disconnected from the rest of the universe. In fact, they feel connected to every living being. They're in touch with their true self and realize that every other living being also has the same true self: all being manifestations of ONE!

Q: But aren't humans social animals? Don't we need each other?

A: In the grip of the Acquired Self, you socialize with people who have something in common with you, such as culture, customs, beliefs, values, race, religion, political and social ideas. In this way, your Acquired Self relates to another Acquired Self and the two strengthen each other. Even when you meet people with a different type of Acquired Self, you try to find some common ground, so you can then socialize. However, if you or the other person leaves the turf of common ground, the socialization often turns into a verbal battle and occasionally turns physical as well.

What we call socialization is actually a way for the Acquired Self to feel secure by finding similar Acquired Selves and by fighting those who are different. In this way, you find and live with Acquired Selves with similar composition. Then you start believing that you need each other to survive. It's true that the Acquired Self needs other similar Acquired Selves to strengthen and survive.

On the other hand, when you are free of your Acquired Self, you don't find it necessary to socialize. The *psychological neediness* to socialize is not there any more. When you meet another person, you don't look at him as friend or enemy. You don't judge him based on his religion, race, culture, political or social beliefs. The psychological need to seek his friendship or to overcome him is not there at all. You have no selfish motives. You look at him simply as another human being.

The socialization that arises out of the True Self is completely different from the one that arises out of the Acquired Self.

Chapter 14

Ego

What is ego? In its common usage the word ego implies "being special." A person is said to have ego if he thinks he is *special and better than others*. However, that person usually doesn't think that he has ego. People usually think of themselves as accomplished, successful, gifted or blessed. These terms are quite flattering compared to "ego" which carries a negative connotation. In fact, these are the same traits of personality.

With rare exceptions, everyone has ego. Everyone feels special or wants to be special in one way or another.

Some examples:

- "I'm" special because "I'm" rich.
- "I'm" special because "I'm" poor.
- "I'm" special because "I'm" famous.
- "I" feel special because "I'm" pretty.
- "I'm" special because "I" survived cancer.
- "I'm" special because "I'm" a spiritual teacher.
- "I'm" special because "I'm" a doctor and "I" heal people.

- "I'm" special because "I'm" a victim of social injustice.

You also may feel special by associating with a special person, place or ideology.

Some examples:

- "I'm" special because "I" know a famous person.
- "I'm" special because "I" carry a prestigious triple platinum credit card.
- "I'm" special because "I" went to a prestigious university.
- "I'm" special because "I" have an impressive degree.

Then there are collective egos. You feel special because you belong to a famous, prestigious, desirable place, group or community.

Some examples:

- I'm" special because "I" live in a certain country, city or neighborhood.
- "I'm" special because "I" belong to a certain social, political or religious organization.
- "I" feel special because "My" ancestors were so great.
- "I" feel special because "I" can speak three languages.
- "I" feel special because "I'm" so cultured.

Often you feel special because of your possessions.

<u>Some examples</u>

- "I" feel special because "I" own a special car.
- "I" feel special because "I" own special jewelry.
- "I" feel special because "I" have such an unique pet.
- "I'm" special because "I" own special antique items that very few people have.
- "I" feel special because of certain clothes "I" wear.

Have you noticed ego revolves around "I"? When you totally identify with "I, My, Me, Mine," you're in the grip of ego. *Your self image is your ego and your self image is "I, My, Me, Mine." That's who you think you are.*

Then all your life, you're either enhancing or defending your ego. In doing so, you create a huge amount of stress for yourself and others. What a waste of your life!

Is it possible to be free of ego? If you sincerely want to be free of ego, you need to look at this question deeply, without any mental rationalization. Use simple logic and you will find the answer.

The Root Cause of Ego

Use logic and you'll find that "I, My, Me, Mine" lies at the root of your ego. As observed earlier, "I, My, Me, Mine" is the axis of your Acquired Self. As you grow up, it simply gets bigger and bigger.

Your Society Monster is the creator of your "I, My, Me and Mine." It teaches you the concepts of *competition* and *comparison* which lie at the root of ego. *"I am better than the others because of so and so."* The Society Monster provides you with plenty of reasons to feel better than others. These ego-maker concepts include wealth, success, fame, knowledge, culture, genealogy, heritage, possessions, looks, appearances, religious, political and social clubs, etc.

Locked in the prison of ego, you feel quite miserable. On the surface, you're accomplished, famous and successful, but deep inside you feel empty, jealous and irritated. When society makes you feel special by acknowledging your success, your heroic actions or your special talents, you get a momentary thrill and excitement, but then it fades away... And you want more. You are never satisfied. You can't get enough praise, validation or recognition. You always want more.

Society of course, can't provide you with praise and recognition all the time. Often, it starts criticizing you as well. First it builds you up and then it brings you down. Then you feel miserable. You want others, especially your close friends and family members, to like you for your accomplishments and achievements. Instead, they generally stop liking you because they don't approve of the way you act under the influence of your

110

ego.

You don't see it that way. You think they're jealous of your success. You often surround yourself with a new set of friends who praise your success. However, inside you keep hurting. You know that these new friends are actually fair-weather friends.

You wish your old friends and family members would praise you the way your new friends do. Meanwhile, your old friends and family members wish that you'd quit being an *egocentric maniac* and come back to your senses. The drama goes on and creates a lot of pain and suffering on both sides. Many people resort to alcohol, drugs and a lot of other escapes discussed earlier.

After years of emotional suffering, you decide to "be successful" at relationships, because you hate to be unsuccessful at anything. You may read some books or get advice from professionals. You may even go to a workshop or two and learn a few techniques. However, in the end, nothing seems to work. *No one seems to fully understand you or appreciate you for who you are and what you have done for others! People are just so ungrateful and take you for granted, etc.*

An egocentric person is in the total grip of his own Acquired Self. He interacts with the world from the virtual castle of his own grandiosity. Why and how is this castle of grandiosity built? The Acquired Self builds this virtual castle in the pursuit of

111

emotional security. It wants to suppress the fire of insecurity and worthlessness. It wants to be someone that everyone praises, validates and acknowledges instead of mocking, humiliating or criticizing.

For example, as a child or as a teenager you were subjected to comparison or criticism by some authority figure, such as your mother or your teacher. You felt the pain of humiliation and worthlessness. You also probably felt that you didn't deserve it. They were simply being mean to you. These thoughts of meanness and unfairness provoked intense anger inside you. All of these thoughts and emotions get stored in your memory as a constant nagging voice of criticism. Memories are part of your Acquired Monstrous Self and give rise to constant painful feelings of worthlessness and anger.

You may or may not be aware of these humiliating experiences any more. Some of these experiences, especially from early childhood, may have been forgotten. However, in your subconscious mind, these experiences are very much alive.

From these humiliating experiences comes another inner thought, "I'll never be humiliated again" or "I'll prove them wrong!" This inner thought becomes your drive to succeed in the world. It makes you work hard. You accomplish a lot, become successful and earn a lot of money and respect.

You get strongly attached to "success," as it validates you and provide a momentary band-aid on the old, but very much alive, wound of humiliation and anger. Attached to your success, you develop a big ego. On the surface you are accomplished and successful, but inside you still feel worthless, humiliated, angry and dissatisfied.

You keep working harder and harder, making more and more money, having more recognition and more power. This makes you more egocentric. You expect and hope that now you will never be humiliated again because you are so successful and powerful. However, inside you continue to feel dissatisfied, insecure, worthless, irritated and angry.

Then, a little thing triggers your inner anger to the surface. You are easily annoyed and have outbursts of anger over things that wouldn't bother other people - things such as someone not agreeing with you or making an innocent, unflattering remark. Why does this trigger your anger? Because you expect them to acknowledge and validate your success. When they don't, you feel like they are criticizing you and you over-react with all your piled up anger. This behavior causes you to lose some true friends. You want validation from your friends, but your actions push away your true friends. How ironic!

You keep proving to others and yourself over and over again how great you are, but it's never enough to heal your inner wound of worthlessness, unfairness and anger.

In your personal life, any minor disagreement with your spouse or children may send your monster into a rage. You don't

113

like this hot temper, but you can't help it. You don't even have a clue where it's coming from.

Actually, the more successful you become, the bigger your ego becomes and the more easily you get angry over little things.

Some people may not have gone through (or may not remember) humiliating experiences. However, they (their Acquired Self) learn from the Society Monster that success, money, power or connections with powerful people are very important to live a "successful life" and they start believing in this delusion. The Society Monster validates these concepts all the time. You (your Acquired Self) get praise and validation through your success, accomplishments, money, power, possessions, looks, etc. Each time it gets validated, its inner insecurity temporarily subsides, so it feels thrilled and excited. Unfortunately, all of this vanishes quickly and then it wants more... And the circus goes on!

Ego can take another form that most people are unaware of. Many people get attached to failures, losses and misery either due to their own experiences (losses in competition and comparison) or collective losses of their collective identity (such as a religious, cultural or political groups). Then they (their Acquired Self) feel *special* in being a failure or miserable... the famous "Martyr Syndrome."

Your Acquired Self gets validation from the Society

114

Monster in the form of knowledge of history (how great your ancestors were, what great sacrifices, losses and humiliations they endured). It also gets validation from books of self improvement that tell you that all evils of the world originate from power, money and sex and if you got rid of these, then you'll be a pious person, a better person as *compared* to those who are wealthy, powerful and sexually desirous.

True Freedom from Ego

The realization that it is your Acquired Self, and not your True Self, who creates your ego has the power to free you from your ego. *Your Acquired Self is always insecure.* Why? Because it is *virtual, unreal and* really does not exists at all. Hence, it is insecure. So it seeks virtual security by being *better* than others, by being *special.* The Society Monster provides it with a number of ideas on how to be *special.* And that's how your Acquired Self is able to live inside you.

It is your Acquired Self, your conditioned mind, who generates memories of every event. That's how it keeps them alive and it calls it My past. The Collective Society Acquired Self (Society Monster) operates exactly in the same fashion and creates a collective human past in the form of knowledge of history. By keeping the past alive, the Acquired Self keeps all the pains of humiliation, worthlessness and unfairness alive and builds a wall of defensive mechanisms around them. These defensive mechanisms, such as competition and comparison, make you respectable, successful or pious in the eyes of the

115

world. Your Acquired Self loves these mechanisms because it gets its validation through these mechanisms. That's why it never lets go of comparison and competition.

Now what happens if you fully understand all of the convoluted working of your Acquired Self? Obviously, you will want to *dissociate* yourself from your Acquired Self and with that, your ego automatically vanishes. You realize there is no need to hold on to "your past," because it's not real: it's not happening any longer.

The Past lives only in your head. In reality, it does not exist. At the present moment, no one is criticizing you or humiliating you through comparison or subjecting you to unfairness. *It happened, but it is not happening at this moment.* No need to build up walls of defensive mechanisms.

You may feel all the piled up emotional pain rushing to your eyes and pouring down in the form of tears. Feel all of this pain, but also realize that no one is humiliating you at this very moment. Therefore, you don't need approval, praise or validation from others. You realize that you don't need to feel better than others. You realize *life is not a race. Life is to live*!

Everyone is a human being. No one is better than the other and there is no *need* to be better than others. This is the end of the *ego*.

Chapter 15

Greed

What is greed? Wanting more, isn't it? Some people want more wealth, some want more power, some want more fame, some want more recognition, etc. In this way, everyone is greedy, with very few exceptions.

People see greed in others, but not in themselves. We easily point fingers at someone else, but forget to see our own greed. The degree of greed may vary, but almost everyone is greedy in some way.

What happens when someone is greedy? "Wanting more" is the opposite of contentment, isn't it? *You can never be content if you are greedy*. Wanting more causes lack of contentment. This leads to a constant urge to be doing something... a state of agitation with no rest and no peace. Most people on the planet suffer from this psychological ailment. They feel rushed, pushed, agitated, restless and nervous. Many develop insomnia, headaches, anxiety and nervousness.

By continuously doing, you may achieve a lot: accumulate a lot of money or earn great fame, but inside, you're a nervous wreck. To relax, you often turn to escapes as discussed earlier.

Because you can make a lot of money from endless doing, you can afford many types of escapes such as vacationing at expensive hide-outs, partying, alcohol, drugs, etc. In order to pay for these expenses, you justify your constant doing: a self-fulfilling prophecy.

The Society Monster coined a sugar coated phrase for this behavior: "Work Hard and Play Hard." These people end up in a cycle of constant doing, constant restlessness, escapes, excessive spending and back to constant doing to earn more. The Society Monster considers these people successful, accomplished, high achievers and rewards them generously with praise, validation and recognition.

However, on the inside, these people have so much tension that it sometimes becomes unbearable for them to live with themselves. This is one of the causes of suicide. They often spend a lot of time in psychiatrists' offices. Many are on sleeping pills, headache medications and anti-anxiety drugs. Most have terrible personal relationships. The only relationship they know and connect with is to money, fame and power.

Greedy people suffer from enormous inner tension and agitation, which often gives rise to ailments such as headaches, insomnia, nervousness and anxiety. They have no clue why they develop these symptoms. They see their doctors who treat their symptoms with various medications. No one looks at the root cause. Therefore, the illness continues and with time, usually gets worse. These people often develop high blood pressure, diabetes, heart attacks, strokes, dementia, and autoimmune disorders such as thyroiditis, rheumatoid arthritis, lupus, irritable bowel syndrome, etc.

Is Greed Human Nature?

Is it possible to be free of greed? The Society Monster tells you that it's impossible to be free of greed because "it's human nature." Is it really human nature?

If you want to discover true human nature, you need to examine newborn babies before they are conditioned by society. When I look at newborn babies, I don't see a shred of greed. Once their stomach is full, they don't ask for more. They don't say, "Mom, that was yummy. I want more." If you force them to drink more milk once their stomach is full, they will regurgitate. "Wanting more" simply does not exist. That's why they are so content and peaceful. Therefore, it's logical to conclude that *greed is not human nature.*

Greed is not human nature. However, it is the nature of the Acquired Self, downloaded into you by society's Collective Acquired Self. That's why society misidentifies greed as human nature. Of course, to the Society Monster, it is human nature.

The Root Cause of Greed

So why does a non-greedy, contented human being

119

becomes so greedy? What happens?

As we observed earlier, as a baby grows, it starts to acquire another psychological self, what we can call the Acquired Self. Psycho-social conditioning is a big part of it. During psycho-social conditioning, *competition and comparison* are drilled into the developing Acquired Self. You see it everywhere; at home, at work, at school, at parties, on TV and practically in every walk of life.

When you're in competition, you either win or lose. What happens when you win? You get praise, validation and recognition. For that moment, you're the king of the hill. You have this wonderful feeling – a natural high filled with thrill and excitement. A few moments later, it's gone. You want more of it, but the moment, the occasion has passed. Now you have to work hard to be the "king of the hill" again. It takes a lot of hard work to be the champion, the winner, the outstanding person again.

The more victories you have, the more addicted you become to the momentary thrill and excitement. There is no ending. You simply want more and more and keep working in that pursuit. This is how you become greedy.

A competitive mind never gets enough and therefore, is always dissatisfied. You may be a wealthy, powerful, accomplished person, but inside you are empty, unhappy and dissatisfied.

Dissatisfaction leads to more greed for momentary pleasures and that means you must earn more money, fame, recognition, etc. It's a vicious cycle which often leads to various addictions, such as addiction to work, power, career, etc. You have no time for your family. Consequences: unhappy spouse, unhappy kids and often divorce which causes more emotional pain.

You seek momentary pleasure to curb this pain by engaging more and more into what you know: more pursuit for money, fame and power, etc.

True Freedom from Greed

Most people are greedy, but don't think of them self as greedy. They stay in denial. When restlessness, agitation and nervousness become unbearable, they run to escapes conveniently created by the Society Monster. In this way, the architects of greed, the Society Monster and your personal Monster, avoid detection and continue to thrive.

What happens if you don't run away from greed and its consequences? You admit that you're greedy and that's why you are so nervous, restless, agitated and dissatisfied. Then there's a chance that you can go deeper and discover the architect of your greed. Once you identify the root cause of your greed, you can cure it.

Recognizing your greedy nature, as part of your Acquired

Self formed from psycho-social conditioning, can free you from greed. Fully realize in your bones that your True Self, your true human nature, does not know any greed. It is full of contentment and joy. In this way, you can be free of greed, and its consequences, once for all!

Chapter 16

The Cycle of Love and Hate

Have you noticed that love often changes into hate? One day you're so close to someone and then your friendship, relationship falls apart. Friends become enemies. Love changes into hate. For example, the so called love that compels you to get married often changes into hate, resulting in a divorce which of course, feeds more hate. How could someone you loved so deeply and cared for so much become your enemy? But you don't want to think about it. That's why you continue to go through the cycles of friendship–animosity, love-hate, like-dislike. Of course, it creates a lot of psychological suffering for you in the form of sadness, hurt and mistrust. Sometimes you also become angry and even revengeful.

You talk to your friends and family members and tell your side of the story. Usually they agree with you and take your side. After all, that's the sign of a good friend: "To be there for you at your time of need." Remember, "A friend in need is a friend indeed," a phrase drilled into us from our school days.

You may see a counselor or read some book on self-improvement. Often this kind of help tells you *not to hate* anyone because hate is a bad, negative emotion and it is not good for you. Therefore, avoid it. You may even be advised to change your hate into love. Now you try very hard *not to be angry or hateful*, but you can't help it: hate and anger keep coming back. You don't know what to do. You may even start to consider yourself a bad person, as you're harboring hate inside you. In this way, you add *guilt* to your emotional baggage.

Sometimes, you are able to force all these so called negative emotions way deep inside, sometimes into your unconscious mind. On the surface, you may be able to be nice and loving, but you continue to feel an inner sense of irritation. It can easily blow into an explosion of anger and hate over something unrelated to your current situation.

Maybe you read something in the newspaper that bothers you or someone makes an innocent remark that strikes you angrily. You overreact and often have no clue why. You may even become ashamed of your behavior as you have been taught not to be angry. Now you might add *shame* to your emotional mess. You try hard to be a loving person, but keep failing in this pursuit over and over again.

The Root Cause of Love and Hate

Love and hate are concepts drilled into your growing Acquired Self. You start to acquire them in your early childhood from reading fairy tales and watching movies. You continue to acquire them as you grow up, from novels, movies, songs, magazines, etc.

With the background of information about love and hate you have acquired, you start to experiment yourself by interacting with others. And add a huge load of love and hate to your growing Acquired Self.

If you truly want to be rid of the cycle of love and hate, you need to find its root cause. First of all, you don't need to run away from your emotion of love or hate. See what happens if you don't run away from your emotions. For instance, if you feel hate, then admit that you are hateful. Stay there, feel the emotion and go deeper. "Who is this inside me who is hateful?" Or if you feel love and attraction for a person, also ask the same question. "Who is this inside me who is feeling attraction and love?" Only then you will find the answer: What is really love and hate? How and why does love changes into hate? How and why do friendships change into animosity?

Use logic and you'll find that love and hate are two sides of the same coin. The root cause of love and hate is "I, Me, My, Mine" Syndrome. Let's examine how it works.

"I, Me, My, Mine" creates positive and negative attachments. Positive attachment is called Like/Love and negative attachment is Dislike/Hate.

For example, you get a rat as a pet for your child. It's My rat your child tells her friends. The Rat gets a name and is pampered. It has its own special cage, food and toys. You and your child feed him. It sits in your child's palm and makes your child very happy. Your child gets *positively attached* to My rat. It basically strengthens her sense of her Acquired Self. Then one day, "My" rat dies. Your child is sad at the loss of "My" rat. Why? Because a part of your child's Acquired Self feels bruised and hurt. The stronger the positive attachment, the more you hurt at the loss. This is the basis of *sadness* you experience at the loss of something or someone you are positively attached to.

Now some time later, you hear noise in your attic in the middle of the night. The next morning, you discover rat droppings in the attic. You're afraid of a rat infestation so you decide to get rid of those nasty creatures (negative attachment). You buy traps to kill the rats, but no luck. You get annoyed and frustrated. You end up calling the professionals. At a significant cost, you finally get rid of the rats. You tell your friend what nasty creatures rats are and how much you had to go through to get rid of them. Your friend repeats a story he read in the newspaper about how rats chewed up the electrical wires in some person's attic and caused a lot of problems. You all conclude that rats are indeed something we should all hate.

Now you understand that "I" *love* a rat if it is *My Rat*. It obeys My commands. I am in full control. It makes Me feel special. However, I *hate* a rat if it is *not My Rat*. It is not under My control. It does not obey My commands. It is a potential threat to "My" belongings.

It's pretty clear that it's not about the rat, but about "Me." A rat is a rat, but "I" don't see it that way. It's "My" attachment

126

(positive or negative) that determines whether "I" like/love a rat or dislike/hate a rat.

Another example: You primarily love your pet (positive attachment), say a dog, because it's "Mine." It gives "Me" love. It needs "Me." It makes "Me" feel better. However, let's say your dog also barks loudly at your neighbor taking a peaceful walk every evening. Your neighbor may start to dislike/hate your dog (negative attachment). The dog creates stress for him each time it interrupts his peaceful walk. Then, one day your dog dies of an illness. You miss your dog due to loss of your positive attachment. Actually, your Acquired Self grieves at the loss of a part of it. Your neighbor on the other hand, is relieved of stress due to the loss of his negative attachment.

There is nothing intrinsically good or bad in a person, an animal or an object. It is "I, Me, My, Mine" that determines whether it is good or bad, based upon its own attachment. If "I" am positively attached, I *love* that person, animal, or object. However, if "I" am negatively attached, I *hate* that person, animal or object.

So, why and how does love change into hate? The answer again lies in understanding the "I, Me, My, Mine" Syndrome.

As long as "I" get my psychological, physical, social or financial needs met from another person, "I" love that person. However, the moment "I" don't get my needs met, "I" don't love

127

the other person any more. Furthermore, if "I" perceive the other person to be a potential threat to "Me," I start hating that person. *That's how love changes into hate.*

True Freedom from the Cycle of Love and Hate

Once you have this logical insight about love and hate, you fully understand that "I, Me, My, Mine" Syndrome determines your likes, dislikes, love and hate. You can then rise above it. You can be free of "I, Me, My, Mine" and interact with the world in a different way.

A person, animal or a thing is what it is: It is neither your friend nor your enemy. You don't need any one to validate you, admire you, praise you, support you financially, or meet your social needs. You are free! This is the end of the cycle of love and hate.

True Love

Love is perhaps one of the most commonly used words by humans. There are actually two kinds of love. When most people use the word love, they refer to love arising out of the Acquired Self. This love can readily change into hate. This love is a concept.

There is, however, another kind of love, which never changes into hate. We can call it True Love. This love is not a concept and does not arise from the "I, Me, My, Mine" of the

Acquired Self. It is there when you are free of your Acquired Self. It is not a concept, so you can't grasp it by reading lyrics, poems or books. *The Mind can never know it because it is outside the confines of the mind.*

Q: I want to find love. How can I do it?

A: Take a closer look at the question. "I" has a desire to find love. Who is this "I?" Of course, it is your Acquired Self, who is full of desires. It is always wanting, wishing, desiring. Your Acquired Self wishes to have love, which is a concept, created by the Collective Acquired Self of society. Can you see how the entire question is in the realm of the Acquired Self?

The Collective Acquired Self of society has created all kinds of ways to acquire love. You've probably tried some of those paths, but are still looking for love. The whole world is looking for love. This love of the Acquired Self readily changes into hate. This love is not real love, but a phantom, consisting of certain thoughts which trigger certain emotions.

On the other hand, true love is not a concept. It is not some mental destination that you will one day arrive at by practicing certain techniques. True love is who your True Self is. It is real. In this way, you are Love. You don't need to search for it. All you need to do is to lift the curtain by freeing your self from your Acquired Self. That's all!

129

Chapter 17

The Cycle of Happiness and Sadness

What is happiness and what is sadness? Happiness is a feeling of elation, thrill and excitement and sadness is the opposite: feeling low, down and empty. Sometimes we're happy and at other times, we're sad. We think it's part of life. We also wish to be happy all the time and never be sad. But happiness is momentary and fleeting. Sooner or later, we fall in the dark hole of sadness, which is also temporary. We continue to ride the rollercoaster of elation and depression.

In order to run away from sadness, you may read some book on self-improvement or spirituality and find a phrase like "this too shall pass." Of course, eventually sadness passes away. Then, you may get a wave of happiness. You forget about "this too shall pass." You want happiness to last forever. Of course, happiness also passes away. You get confused. Why does happiness have to pass away? "I don't understand it" you tell yourself. You ask your spiritual teacher or guru, but still don't find a satisfactory answer. The usual reply is: that's how things are. That's how the universe works. It is the law of nature. These explanations still don't satisfy you. "Why can't everyone be happy forever? Why does happiness have to pass?"

The Root Cause of Happiness and Sadness

In order to find real answers, we need to use our true intelligence: logic without any preconceived notions or ideas. Use logic and look at the cycle of "happiness and sadness" to find answers.

When you're happy, who is really happy? It's the "Me" inside you, isn't it? As we observed earlier, the axis of your Acquired Self, "I, My, Me, Mine" creates positive and negative attachments to people, animals, concepts, ideologies, etc. Positive attachments give you (your Acquired Self) momentary excitement it calls happiness. Loss of positive attachments creates sadness.

For example, you inherit a ring from your beloved grandmother. It's very special to you and has huge sentimental value. You (your Acquired Self) are positively attached to it. To you, it is not a ring any more. It is much more than that. *It is part of who you are.* In fact, it is part of your Acquired Self and your Acquired Self is who you think you are. It makes you *happy.* It gives you pleasure.

Then one day, you lose your precious ring. You search for it and turn the entire house upside down, but can't find it. You (your Acquired Self) feel utterly *sad and unhappy* because you lost a part of yourself.

Another example: You love your looks (positive

132

attachment). Your looks become part of "I, My, Me, Mine." "I am beautiful" you keep telling yourself. You frequently look at the mirror for verification. Your friends and family members also verify that indeed, you are beautiful. Even strangers may validate that you are absolutely beautiful. You get special recognition, special treatment and special comments because you are beautiful. All of these experiences give you momentary thrills you call happiness.

Then you lose your beautiful looks due to aging or illness. The loss of "My beauty" is a big loss for your Acquired Self. That obviously creates a huge amount of *unhappiness and sadness*.

Different people are attached to different things. Most people are attached to money. When you get money, say a bonus at work, a big increase in your stocks or a jackpot at a casino, you feel thrilled and happy. However, when you lose your job, your stocks go down, or you lose money at a casino, you feel unhappy and sad.

Most people are also attached to their friends and some family members. They feel happy when they see their favorite family members and close friends and miss them when they are not around. They are not ordinary people. They are special because they are a part of "Me." When they die, a part of you (actually your "Me," the Acquired Self) dies. A huge loss to your Acquired Self creates extraordinary sadness.

Almost everyone is attached to their health. Some are attached to cars, houses, pets, household items, collectible items,

133

clothes, etc. Some are attached to their jobs, achievements, fame, position, etc. Some are attached to ideologies and philosophies.

All of these attachments become part of "Me." When you have them, these provide you (your Acquired Self) with moments of happiness. Sooner or later, you lose them and when that happens, your Acquired Self feels bruised because a part of "Me" is not there any more. That creates a lot of sadness.

Another way to get trapped in the cycle of happiness and sadness is through "competition." In a competition, you may win and that makes you very *happy* or you may lose, and that makes you very *unhappy*. In a competition, there is almost always a simultaneous winner and a loser, except for when the match ends in a tie. So while a person or a group celebrates victory, the other person or a group grieves their loss. People are so drawn into their victory and happiness that they don't think about the misery of others.

Competition is one of the basic ingredients of all societies. Everyone wants to win and be happy and no one wants to lose and be unhappy. In other words, everyone is positively attached to the concept of winning and negatively attached to concept of losing.

Right from early childhood, you're conditioned to win and never lose. The software of "win or lose" gets downloaded into your Acquired Self at a very early age with the help of video games, athletic games, board games, spelling bee contests and beauty competitions, to name just a few. Each time your Acquired Self, your "I" wins, you (your "I") get happy because your "I" gets validation and praise. And each time it loses, you (your "I") feel sad. Competition gets worse as you grow up. Just look around and you'll see how immersed we are in the game of "win or lose." The whole world is built on it. There are the Olympics, the US Open, Wimbledon, the World Cup and so on. Then there are beauty pageants, talent competitions, entertainment competitions, wrestling competitions, even eating competitions, car races, horse races, dog races etc. These are just a few examples that illustrate how prevalent competition is around the world.

People compete at their homes, at work places, even on the highways. You get so hooked on competition that you compete indirectly, when you're not directly competing for something. For example, you get associated with a sports team or a political party. When you positively associate with any person or a group, it becomes part of "I, My, Me, Mine." Then the victory or defeat of that person, team, party or group becomes your victory or defeat. That's why each time your sports team or your political party wins, you feel happy and each time they lose, you feel sad. You feel happy if your favorite singer or actor wins a prestigious competition televised all over the world and feel sad if they lose.

People compete even when they are socializing. Everyone wants to win their argument and be happy. In bars and clubs, people compete for their sex-mates.

Then there is a collective game of win or lose in the form of wars between various groups and countries.

True Freedom from the Cycle of Happiness and Sadness

Use logic and you will see that the game of winning and losing is simply a concept, a mental abstraction and is virtual… But you think it's real. That's the illusion. It's only in your head in the form of thoughts, that's all. Your mind thinks it's real because it has acquired this concept and made it a part of "Me." In addition, you see everyone else talking about it. Of course, you start believing in it!

Throughout your life, you continue to go through this circus of "happiness and sadness" over and over again. Your Society Monster, in the form of your family, friends, books and teachers, continue to reinforce this concept of "happiness and sadness" as if this is something normal and nothing can be done about it.

Now imagine what happens if a person, whose mind has *not* been conditioned, watches sports. What he sees is that a number of people chase and bounce a ball (basketball), carry a ball (rugby), or hit a ball (soccer, baseball, cricket, tennis, golf, ping-pong), etc. He may find it amusing. In the end, he is neither happy nor unhappy, as the concept of victory or defeat doesn't exist in his mind.

Happiness and unhappiness are creations of the human
136

mind. It has nothing to do with nature. Now imagine a person whose mind has *not* been conditioned, who does not have the virtual "I, My, Me, Mine" sitting in his mind; who does not have any attachments. Will he be in the grip of the cycle of happiness and sadness? Of course not!

It is clear that happiness and sadness is a creation of the conditioned mind, the Acquired Self. Freedom from the Acquired Self automatically frees you from the cycle of happiness and sadness

Q: Who would I be without happiness and sadness? Aren't these emotions part of human nature?

A: As we observed earlier, happiness and sadness are created by the Acquired Self, through competition and comparison and through attachments. Therefore, to the Acquired Self, this becomes human nature. When you fully identify with your Acquired Self, you believe happiness and sadness are human nature... And the Society Monster validates your belief.

It is only when you're free of your Acquired Self that you can see the real face of happiness and sadness. You realize that these emotions are the nature of the Acquired Self, but not that of the True Self. Free of the Acquired Self, you experience what we can call "true joy."

137

True Joy

There is a joy that has no opposite. There is always joy, but never any unhappiness or sadness. This true joy does not arise from any concepts. It is not a part of the conditioned mind. You cannot acquire it. It is not a part of your Acquired Self. In fact, your conditioned mind (your Acquired Self) eclipses this true joy that has resided inside you since your birth. It is part of your True Self.

You see it in newborn babies. Once a baby's basic physical needs are met (a full stomach, a clean diaper and a warm blanket), it is there. It shines through the baby's face. It's there before a baby is attached to anything such as toys or parents. The baby doesn't have to score victories to be happy.

This true joy is still in you. It is not a concept. The Mind can never know it, because it is not a concept. You can feel it once you are free of your conditioned mind, your Acquired Self.

Q: There is so much unhappiness in the world. I want to change the world. Therefore, I joined a special organization. Isn't that wonderful?

A: Observe who this "I" is who wants to change the world. You're in the grip of "I, My, Me, Mine," aren't you?

When you say I want to change the world, what you really mean is somewhat like this: "I've" figured out how to change the world and lessen all the sufferings of mankind; See how great "I" am? "I'm" convinced it will work. "I" know "I'm" right.

Everyone seems to have some formula for how to change the world. They're all convinced they're right and others are wrong. They join various social and religious organizations, which often fight with each other, to get *more* funding, to get *more* recognition, to get *more* fame. Within each organization, people fight for various positions, or to prove their ideas right and others' wrong.

If you look with logic, many people who try to change the world are in the grip of greed and self-righteousness, in their collective as well as individual egos.

Have you ever wondered why someone really wants to change the world? The usual answer, of course, is that there is so much suffering in the world... But why is there so much unhappiness in the world? Isn't unhappiness created by greed, selfishness, ego, anger, self-righteousness, grievances, hate and fear? Therefore, doesn't it make sense to free the world of these nasty roots of all unhappiness? Isn't your inner world full of greed, ego, selfishness, anger, self-righteousness, grievances, hate, and fear?

Your inner world is the mirror image of the outer world that the collective human mind has created. So, why not start by

139

cleaning your inner world? In order to truly change the outer world, you need to change your inner world first!

Chapter 18

Complaining

Have you observed how people complain all the time? Complaining is so prevalent that most people are not even aware they are complaining. It sounds like the normal way of thinking.

<u>Some examples:</u>

I don't like this weather.
I don't like my job.
I don't like living in this area.
I don't like this culture.
I don't like all this greed.
I don't like this music.
I don't like my looks.
I don't like my husband.
I don't like what's happening in the world.
I didn't like the service I got.
I was treated so badly.
I didn't like the food that was served.
I didn't like my history teacher.

Who is complaining?

Have you ever wondered when someone is complaining, who is actually complaining? If you pay attention, you will realize it is always "I" who complains. Who is this "I?" Isn't it your Acquired Self? It does *not like* what is happening or what has already happened. Often it does *not like* certain concepts.

When it says "I don't like," it is *judging*. Where does this *judging* come from? From psychosocial conditioning. From early childhood, your Acquired Self learns to *judge every person, object and situation based on the information and concepts already stored in it.*

Resistance, Non-Acceptance

By complaining, your Acquired Self actually puts up a wall of *resistance, non-acceptance* of *what is* or *what was.* You may hear yourself saying, "*It should not have happened,*" or "*It should not be happening.*"

The expression of this *non-acceptance* varies from person to person, depending upon the overall make-up of the Acquired Self. Some people may use strong negative words in a loud voice, while others may put a *sarcastic* tone to it. Some others may politely express it in their *chit-chatting* with their friends. Some may not express it verbally at all but keep talking about it in their *head.* Really, it does not matter how your Acquired Self expresses it.

Each time you complain, verbally or mentally in your head, your Acquired Self triggers negative emotions with serious consequences for your body. By complaining, your Acquired Self is trying to assert itself as being *right* and someone else as *wrong*.

For example, you tell your story to your friends, trying to get sympathy from their Acquired Selves which they gladly provide. In addition, they reinforce your *complaint* with their own stories. Soon you have several stories centered on how *everyone else is wrong*. In this way, the Acquired Selves of all of you find something *in common* and feel bonded. In fact, all of you have produced negativity not only for yourself, but also for everyone around you, *a cloud of negativity*. This is how *victim mentality* is produced.

Sometimes, it may not be your own experience, but actually someone else's experience that you have never met. Next time, in a social situation, just examine how one person starts complaining in a polite way. For example, someone shares some news she read in the newspaper or heard on TV centered around someone's complaining. Soon several Acquired Selves engage by telling their own stories or stories they read or watched on the news. If you pay attention you can actually sense the *heaviness of the field of negative emotions*.

Freedom from Complaining

Use logic and you clearly see you cannot change what has already happened or is already here. Then you can be free of complaining. For example, your complaining about the weather is not going to change it. Once you fully realize it is your Acquired Self who loves to complain and it does not serve any purpose, you will be free of complaining.

It doesn't means you can't point it out if something is wrong. Once you are free of your *habit of complaining*, you can clearly mention your *point of view* as a matter of fact. This type of action does not arise out of negativity and does not have a fighting tone to it. You may be surprised to see that this non-negative *tone* actually is much more effective than the negative tone.

Chapter 19

Lying

People lie all the time. Ironically, everyone preaches others not to lie, but they themselves continue to lie. People can often clearly see when others lie and condemn them for it. However, they don't think it's so bad when they lie themselves. Interesting, isn't it? They quickly judge a liar as a bad person, but rationalize their own lying, often as a necessity under the circumstances or because of this or that excuse.

The Root Cause of Lying

Have you ever wondered why someone lies, despite knowing that lying is a bad thing? The pull towards lying is so strong that it overrides all the teachings against it. In order to understand "lying," we need to go deeper rather than simply calling it a bad behavior and passing judgment on it.

Why do people lie? Mostly because they are afraid of being caught. And why are we afraid of being caught? Because we will be punished if we get caught. If you have done something "wrong," you know you will be punished for your action. Obviously you don't want to be punished, therefore you lie.

Who is this in you who lies? It's your Acquired Self, isn't

145

it? You are not born with it. You acquire the concepts of "bad behavior, punishment and avoiding pain and suffering." As a result of these concepts, you start lying.

For example, as a child you did something which your parents thought was wrong. Let's say you hid your brother's shoes. They asked if you did it and you said, "yes." Subsequently, you got punished for it. Your memory stored the entire event as a pain arising out of admission of wrong doing. Your mind learns from its mistake and generates another thought in your subconscious: I will avoid pain by never admitting any wrong doing. In school, you do wrong things, but never admit it. You not only get away with your pranks, but may also be praised by other kids who start to think of you as *a sneaky genius.* You may become a habitual liar. You create a monster of never admitting any wrong-doing.

Actually, the Society Monster often further enhances your lying habits by rewarding some liars as clever men. Many lawyers lie all the time and get paid well for their brilliant work. They also strongly advise you to *never* admit any wrong-doing.

Actually, you feel quite thrilled when you can get away with a wrong-doing. However, sooner or later, you get caught and face punishment. Then you go through painful emotions of anger, guilt and shame. In life, you continue to pile up memories of thrills of getting away with "wrong-doings" and emotional pain arising out of being caught and punished. That's how your Acquired Self works and keeps you trapped in lying.

146

Sometimes, people lie to a person because they think the truth would hurt them. Actually, sooner or later that person finds out the truth and gets hurt even more. And you will feel embarrassed, guilty and ashamed.

True Freedom from Lying

When you get caught lying, you feel embarrassed, ashamed and guilty. Obviously, it causes a lot of emotional pain for you. Therefore, you try to seek some help, usually in the form of counseling from a friend, from a professional or from a book. It may work for a while, but before you know it you are repeating the whole cycle all over again.

Can there be a true freedom from lying? You need to ask this question yourself. My answer is Yes. If you use logic, you realize that lying arises out of the concepts of "bad behavior, punishment, and avoiding pain and sufferings." These concepts are drilled into you by society as you grow up.

Where do these concepts come from? If you use common sense, you realize these concepts are a product of the Collective Acquired Self of society, the collective human mind. These concepts are part of the long list of concepts which are simply the byproducts of human civilization: concepts that arose as humans started living together in communities.

So, you should see these concepts for exactly what they

147

are: concepts and no more. Then, you get freedom from the tight grip of these concepts. You no longer believe in these concepts to be the ultimate Truth. In this very basic realization, you become free of the tight grip of the concepts of bad behavior, punishment and avoidance of sufferings.

With this realization, you are no longer in the grip of concepts, which are part of your Acquired Self. Once you are free of your Acquired Self, you are free of selfishness, ego, greed, self-righteousness and insecurity. Only then, your actions arise which are not bad at all. Then is there is no fear of being caught and obviously there is no need to Lie.

Chapter 20

Bias and Prejudice

What is bias and prejudice? In simple terms, we are biased or prejudiced when we judge things, people or events with preconceived ideas.

With rare exceptions, everyone is biased, aren't they? We look at everything through the filters of information stored in our mind. That's why we are constantly looking at things, interpreting events, judging people with bias, with prejudice. Almost all of our experiences are tainted with information stored in our mind. There are hardly any original, unconditioned, untainted experiences.

Amazingly most people think they are not biased or prejudiced! Why? Because they also have this notion that bias and prejudice are bad qualities. Therefore, no one likes to be called biased even though everyone, with rare exceptions, is biased.

If we want to be free of bias and prejudice, isn't it logical to look at bias and prejudice without any preconceived ideas of it being bad? Once we can admit without being ashamed that we are biased or prejudiced, we can go deeper and find out the root cause of our bias and prejudice. Only then, there is a chance that we can truly be free of bias and prejudice.

149

What is the Root Cause of Bias and Prejudice?

Why are we biased and prejudiced? Obviously we interpret everything, judge every person and experience every event through the filters of information stored in our mind. We have piles and piles of information about everything one can imagine stored in our mind. We call it *knowledge*! The more knowledgeable, the better we are! It is obvious that this *knowledge is the basis of our bias and prejudice.*

Where does this knowledge come from and why are we so thirsty for knowledge? It goes back to our early childhood when we are told by our loved ones, our parents, our teachers, to acquire as much knowledge as possible.

Initially, we are reluctant to acquire it, but we are forced to learn it. We are punished if we do not acquire knowledge and rewarded if we do. The entire system of education is about acquiring knowledge, isn't it? The tool of punishments and rewards works well to condition us. In addition, we also get all sorts of additional information from our parents: What are our roots, our values, our traditions, our beliefs, what is right, what is wrong. The conditioned mind is our Acquired Self.

Slowly our Acquired Self develops such an insatiable appetite for acquiring information that we feel restless and bored if we are not engaged in acquiring more information. We start and end our day by acquiring information through newspapers, the

150

internet and TV. The mental activity of acquiring more and more information seems to be an essential part of living. Without acquiring more knowledge, it seems we will not be able to survive. It is true that our *Acquired Self needs more and more information to thrive or it may perish.* When we are fully identified with our Acquired Self, as most of us are, we consider knowledge an essential part of us.

Most of the information stored in our mind is in fact, others' opinions and points of view - that's all. It is not based on our own experience. But in the grip of the Acquired Self, we don't see it that way. We take it as the truth. We don't even realize that there are many different stories about the same event, person or thing. *The Acquired Self is very illogical.* Every Acquired Self believes that the information it contains is true, especially if it is of special interest to it, such as some political or religious information. That's why people get into heated arguments. Often, it leads to verbal or even physical violence.

True Freedom from Bias and Prejudice

To be free of bias and prejudice, we need to be free of our Acquired Self! Then we realize that all the information we acquire is simply information - usually others' opinions - and that's all!

We can experience things as they really are, only if we are free of preconceived ideas, free of our Acquired Self. Then we see a person as a human being, a manifestation of life, not as

151

white, black, brown, Christian, Muslim, Hindu, Jewish, English, Hispanic, American, French or Chinese. Then we see a bird as another manifestation of life, and not as a blue-jay, eagle or hummingbird. Then we see a tree as another manifestation of life, and not as a pine, oak or mango tree. We look at sunset without interpreting it as sunset and without comparing it to another sunset.

Once we are free of the all of the stored information, we can have original, fresh, unconditioned experiences. Prejudice and bias automatically dies.

Q: It sounds great, but in reality, how can I function without all of the information and knowledge.

A: This is how the Acquired Self puts up resistance: "Oh! It sounds good but I'm not buying it because I can't function without it. Therefore, I'm fine the way I am. I don't want any change."

It is true that your Acquired Self cannot function without information and knowledge. And when you totally identify with the Acquired Self, you feel the same way.

But what happens when you are free of your Acquired Self? Then, you are totally free of the filters created by the stored up information and knowledge. You experience life the way it is. In addition, you utilize your Acquired Self as a tool to function in society. In this way, you become the master of your Acquired Self, instead being enslaved by it.

Staying in touch with who you really are changes even your Acquired Self. Then automatically, you function in the world in an effective way without producing stress for yourself or others.

For example, when you're in touch with your True Self, you automatically look at every human being as a human being - not as a white, brown, black, Christian, Jewish, Buddhist, Hindu or Muslim. You automatically become free of bias and prejudice. Then, your interactions in every day life are actually more productive and effective.

Chapter 21

Jealousy

What is jealousy? Jealousy is a gnawing emotion. It kills any peace of mind you have. A jealous person is in constant psychological pain. Even worse, he can't even admit to being jealous, because it's bad to be a jealous person. It's a sign of failure and bad character to be jealous, isn't it?

The Root Cause of Jealousy

Why do you get jealous? If you pay attention, you realize jealousy arises out of your own mind. Watch your mind and you may hear this kind of inner voice: "I deserve what he has. Why him and not me?" ... Or "Why did she get the praise and not me?" ... Or "I'm the one who really deserves to have a loving spouse, mansion, fame, praise, validation and recognition. Why does that person have everything and not Me? The other person is a winner and I'm a loser." There is a deep seated sense of *lack of praise* and *unfairness* when you are jealous.

It's all about "I, My, Me, Mine," isn't it? It's your Acquired Self who is jealous. The Acquired Self is conditioned to be *competitive*. It wants to win and never lose. It wants to be praised, validated and acknowledged by others. Therefore, it works hard to win, to be better than others and *expects* the praise, validation and acknowledgement of others. Why? Because the Society Collective Acquired Self promises it success, praise and validation if it works hard, follows the rules and is an honest person. However, when it doesn't get what it expects, it gets deeply hurt.

True Freedom from Jealousy

As long as you identify with your Acquired Self, you will continue to *expect* praise from others. If others praise someone else, you'll stay in the tight grip of jealousy.

In the grip of the Acquired Self, you continue to *expect* success due to your hard work. You *expect* your wife to love you because you love her. You *expect* your children to love you because you love them. When your expectations are not met, you are hurt and jealous of those who are unfairly getting what you deserve.

The moment you realize that you are not who thought you were, you become free of the neediness to be praised and acknowledged. You are not your Acquired Self. You realize that your True Self existed before you were lured into the game of competition and comparison. You realize the conceptual nature of "win and lose, praise and reward." There is nothing real in these concepts. You become free of the neediness to be praised, loved, validated or acknowledged by others. That's how jealousy simply ends.

156

Chapter 22

Addictions

Addiction affects most of us to a more or less degree. It is only when it becomes excessive and undesirable that we as a society call it addiction. Addictions can take various forms: compulsive eating, smoking, excessive work, excessive TV watching, excessive video games, excessive golfing, excessive vacationing, excessive partying, excessive alcohol, excessive gambling, excessive illegal drugs, excessive computer use, etc.

It's interesting to note that the Society Monster has singled out certain excessive behaviors as *addictions* and others as *accomplishments*. For example, a business man seeking pleasure in making more and more money and not spending time with his wife and children is called an accomplished, honorable person. He may have an affair which leads to divorce and huge emotional pain for his family, but he is still an accomplished person. On the other hand, a person seeking excessive pleasure in illegal drugs is considered a failure and a bad person. If you think logically, they are both addicted, one to money and the other to illegal drugs.

The Root Cause of Addiction

If you want to be rid of any addiction, first you need to find out the root cause of your addiction, don't you? In most cases, *competition, comparison, judging and guilt* are at the root of addictions. In the game of *competition*, you either win or lose. If you win, you get *thrill, excitement and pleasure.* But it is short-lived and you want you more of it.

What happens if you lose in a competition? It leads to emotions of unworthiness and sadness. At times, it also causes a sense of *unfairness, self-pity, bitterness, anger and jealousy.* You also want to win next time. You want to take *revenge* and humiliate the other person, party or team, etc.

Comparison always makes "someone better" or "someone worse." Judging is based on the concepts downloaded into our Acquired Self, such as the concepts of beauty and ugliness, intelligence and stupidity, good and bad, wealth and poverty, etc.

Now what happens when you are told that you are "better than" or you are "the best" or "the most beautiful?" Obviously, you feel praised, validated and special. You want more of these compliments.

What happens when you are told that you are "worse than" or "the worst" or even "dumb and stupid?" Obviously you feel worthless, humiliated and sad. You definitely do not want to hear those kinds of comments!

Judging also gives rise to *"guilt."* As we observed earlier in the book, the root cause for guilt is self-criticism, which is the result of the "book" of values, traditions, morality and ethics downloaded into your Acquired Self, all of which are concepts created by your society. You judge yourself (and everyone else) through the filters of these concepts. What happens if on some occasion, or in a certain situations, you can't live up to these concepts? Obviously, you feel guilty for the rest of your life.

In life, you sometimes win and at other times lose; sometimes you are praised and at other times criticized. Sometimes you can live up to the standards and at other times, you fail. In this way, you accumulate a huge pile of psychological burden through the game of *competition, comparison* and *judging*.

Victories, praises and validations bring momentary "thrill and excitement" to your Acquired Self. *And it wants more of it.* It becomes *addicted* to the moments of thrill and excitement. The pursuit of *more* makes you greedy and you are never satisfied. It may be greed for money, power, success, validation, etc.

Therefore, you live in a psychological state of dissatisfaction, agitation and nervousness even when you are winning. Consequently, you may seek out more and more momentary thrills and excitement through recreational drugs, alcohol, gambling, prostitutes, pornography, excessive vacationing, etc.

159

On the other hand, your Acquired Self also holds on to the psychological pains of humiliation, worthlessness, unfairness, anger, revenge and guilt. Your Acquired Self holds onto your experiences of the past as if they are happening right now. This keeps the fire of emotional pains burning.

As this pain becomes intolerable, you seek *pleasure* by running away from these pains. So you hit a bar or a casino, over indulge in your favorite foods, take illegal drugs, do excessive work, watch pornography or light one cigarette after another, etc. However, this pleasure is short lived and soon you are back to your usual state of sadness, unworthiness, jealousy or guilt. Then, you run back to seek more pleasure. The more pain you have, the more you are going to seek pleasure. This obviously leads to *addiction*.

Running away from emotional pain and seeking momentary thrill, excitement and pleasure is the basis of *addiction*.

The outwardly manifestations of addictive behavior vary from person to person. Addiction to alcohol, drugs, food, work, sex, gambling, partying, vacationing, pornography and smoking are some of the manifestations. The consequences can be horrendous and obviously, cause huge stress for you and those around you.

When the monster of addiction is acting out through you,

160

you lose all control. Intellectually, you know that excessive food, cigarettes, alcohol, drugs, sex, etc. are damaging and you should not indulge in them, but you feel helpless in front of this monster. It's as if you have been enslaved by this monster. You feel this *helplessness* inside you, which causes further emotional pain, which makes you want to escape more and the vicious cycle of addiction continues.

Often, you try to keep your addiction to yourself and hide it from others. Why? Because there is a stigma of failure and bad behavior attached to it. You feel *ashamed* of yourself. So you continue to suffer in isolation, by yourself. You start to realize that no one really understands your pain. *Shame* and *Loneliness* get added to the heap of your emotional pain.

Sometime you get enough courage and consult your doctor for help, who conveniently prescribes an anti-anxiety or an anti-depression drug. These medicines provide you with another escape and most people get addicted to them. These medicines often have serious side-effects as well.

The root cause for all this mess, *competition, comparison, judging and guilt,* remain undiagnosed and untreated. Besides, how can it be diagnosed when doctors and drug companies are also suffering from the same illness of competition, comparison and judging?

Everyone around you is in the same boat. You believe that this is how life is. You see competition, comparison, judging

161

and guilt at the root of the problem, but you presume that this is human nature. "Everyone is doing it, so it must be human nature" you convince yourself. The Society Monster validates your conclusion.

Some people suppress their emotions so deep that on the surface, they feel fine. Usually, they don't even see their addictive behavior as an addiction. For example, a person may not see his excessive working, cigarette smoking, excessive partying, alcohol consumption or vacationing as a problem, although people around him can clearly see the problem.

True Freedom from Addictions

First of all, be honest to yourself and don't run away from your addiction. Instead, look deeper and only then you can see the mastermind of your addiction: your Acquired Self. Then you realize that you were *not* born with this addiction and this addiction is the result of your psychosocial conditioning, your Acquired Self, the Monster within. With this realization, you can be free from the tight grip of your addiction.

Once you realize that the game of competition, comparison, judging and the "book" of morality, ethics, traditions and values are created by society, the collective human mind, you start to see the true face of these concepts. You realize that these concepts are part of the "nature of the Acquired Self," but *not* the True Self. You realize these concepts are not "true human nature."

You see True Human Nature in newborns. When you observe newborns, you see no competition or comparison, no judging, no morality, ethics, values or traditions.

You realize that goals, achievements, fairness, criticism, judging and obligations, are all concepts drilled into your Acquired Self by the Society Monster.

Thrill, excitement, unworthiness, sadness, jealousy, guilt, loneliness and shame are consequences of these concepts, nothing more! These emotions become part of your Acquired Self. As long as you are in the grip of your Acquired Self, you will continue to hold on to them, no matter, how destructive these emotions are.

You were *not* born with any of these emotions. This logical insight is the beginning of your breaking away from the addictions.

Each time you have the urge to run for your escape in order to seek pleasure to kill your sadness, jitteriness, emptiness, guilt, shame, loneliness or boredom, you will realize that it is your Acquired Self luring you into these escapes. With this wisdom, you will be able to rise above the urge to escape and addiction will loosen its grip on you.

Each time you are free from your Acquired Self, you will find true peace and joy in your own True Self. The more you stay with your True Self, the less likely you will fall into the trap of addictions.

Alertness and awareness about the sneaky nature of your Acquired Self is extremely important. It is not *discipline,* but simple *awareness* about your Acquired Self, the Monster within, that is the key to freedom from addictions.

Discipline makes you feel like you are trying to control your addictions. Sooner or later it fails or you are afraid of it failing or it may surface in another addiction. However, simple awareness of the root cause of addictions frees you from addictions with a sense of release and Aahhh!

Chapter 23

Overeating as an Addiction

Overeating is the true epidemic of our time. It causes weight gain and obesity, with serious health consequences such as diabetes, high blood pressure, cancer, heart attack, stroke, gall stones, low back pain, etc. Most people know these basic facts, but they continue to overeat. Over the years, I have not met a single obese person who does not understand the health hazards of obesity and who does not want to lose weight.

Obese people want to lose weight, but most of them feel they can't do it alone. So they seek out help. A lot of help is available in the form of weight loss programs, diet pills, dietary counseling, etc. However, this type of help works for the short term only. Most people gain back their weight once they are off the program. Obviously, they feel frustrated. They continue to jump from one weight loss technique to another. They go through the cycle of "weight loss and weight gain," and associated "happiness and sadness." Many give up for one reason or another. A lot of people get depressed.

Being an endocrinologist, I frequently see patients with obesity. Here are some of the phrases I hear frequently:
- *"I have no discipline."*

- *"I am such a loser."*
- *"It's all my wife's fault."*
- *"I was doing so well until we went on the trip."*
- *"I will work on it, one day."*
- *"I need to lose 30 pounds for my daughter's upcoming wedding."*
- *"I can't control my eating when I go to parties."*
- *"I work so hard during the day. Then I reward myself in the evening by eating whatever I want."*
- *"I cheat here and there and that's enough to prevent me from losing weight, but I can't help it."*
- *"I know I stuff down my emotions, but I can't help it."*
- *"It seems like I do good for a while, but once I fall off the wagon, I can't get back on my strict regimen."*
- *"Sometimes I feel that I don't care. Then I eat food I know I shouldn't eat."*
- *"I eat excessively under social pressure, although I know better, but I can't help it."*

Most people don't go any deeper than these comments. If you look a little deeper, you'll see it is your Acquired Self, the Monster within, who is sabotaging your plans to lose weight by blaming others and yourself, finding excuses, playing the game of rewards and punishment, etc.

Interestingly, it is your Acquired Self who also makes plans to lose weight by disciplining yourself in one way or another. If you cannot discipline yourself, you find a weight loss program to

166

discipline you, which of course, works for a while, costs a lot of money and then, you are back to your usual state of "lack of discipline." Each time you fall off the wagon, you get more disappointed. Even when you are disciplined, you feel like you are punishing yourself.

The Root Cause of Overeating

In order to be free of overeating, you need to first get to the root of overeating behavior. Why does someone overeat? Look deeper and you'll see that overeating is due to learned habits of eating.

Where do we acquire habits of eating? From home, from school and from society in general, don't we? First, you are downloaded with certain cultural foods as special, important food items. They keep a tight grip on you for the rest of your life. I remember a patient of mine once told me, "Doc, I can't stop eating pizza. I know it's bad for my health, but for God's sake, I'm an Italian. How can I ever stop eating *pizza?!*"

You also learn to eat not only when you are hungry, but also to have fun. All social occasions, including birthdays, weddings, religious, cultural and national holidays are centered around food. That's how you acquire the concept of *"food means fun."* You can't imagine celebrating a certain holiday without the special food items that go with that holiday, no matter how harmful it may be for your health.

You also learn that *food* **equals reward**. You learn the concept that you are blessed if you have plenty of food. Remember your parents telling you, "how lucky you are to have such good food while there are so many hungry children in Africa." In schools, you are often promised ice-cream or some other favorite food if you achieve certain points and grades.

Now what is opposite of reward? Punishment, right? So when you discipline yourself not to eat your favorite food, it's as if you are punishing yourself. Therefore, over the weekend, you have the urge to reward yourself with plenty of your favorite food, no matter how unhealthy it may be. *That's how you get stuck in the cycle of punishment and reward.*

Often people eat to **stuff their stress down**. For example, all day, you work hard, dealing with stressful situations. Finally, you are at home, tired and exhausted from all the craziness that went on at work. You are ready to unwind, relax and enjoy. So what do you do? You go for the food items that you love! "Come on, you deserve to have this **good** time after all the **bad** time you had at work," says your inner voice. This voice is so powerful that you completely ignore what your doctor told you or what you promised yourself last time you weighed yourself.

People often stuff down their frustrations, sadness, loneliness, boredom and guilt with food. Later, they feel even guiltier for breaking their diet. And the vicious cycle goes on.

Society also teaches you to express your love,

friendship and gratefulness through food. These are all concepts, but you start to believe in them as absolutely important things.

Perhaps now you understand why we mostly eat for *psychological and social reasons* and not for *physiological reasons.* That's why we often eat when we are not even hungry, and we continue to eat even when we are no longer hungry.

All of these concept-based eating habits are part of your Acquired Self. As long as you identify with your Acquired Self, you obviously can't get rid of these habits and concepts. For example, how can you ever celebrate a birthday without a cake? As long as you are attached to the concept of birthday, you are going to have a cake, even if you are diabetic or obese.

True Freedom from Overeating

In the grip of the Acquired Self, you will continue to struggle with your weight because the Acquired Self is the root cause of your overeating. You cannot be completely free of your overeating behavior as long as you are in the grip of your Acquired Self. For a while, you may force yourself not to indulge, but sooner or later, you will fail.

Even during your dieting period, you will feel pressured from your self imposed discipline and you will feel deprived. This makes you irritable and affects your behavior towards others. You overreact to simple things. You often don't realize the true cause of your snappy behavior. You always blame it on others, instead of your self created prison of discipline.

Use common sense, and realize that the root cause of your overeating problem lies inside you: your Acquired Self. Be free of your Acquired Self, and you will be free of your eating habits.

Remember the example I quoted earlier - my patient who would not stop eating pizza because he was Italian? I told him that he should tell himself that he is *not* Italian. The fact is that he *was not* Italian when he was born. He was *made* Italian by his parents. He could have been made French, Spanish, Indian, etc. as well. It is simple conditioning by our parents that makes us Italian, German, English, Christian, Muslim, Jewish, Hindu, etc. - all of which are concepts, right? These concepts become part of our Acquired Self. Then we start to believe them as if they were true.

To the Acquired Self, every concept is important because concepts are an important part of it. In reality, concepts are simply concepts and should be treated just like that. *Once my patient could see the conceptual nature of being Italian, he was able to be rid of this concept and with that his lifelong attachment to pizza went away.*

The realization that concepts are just concepts will free you from their strong hold on you. Then you realize that:

170

- You are neither Italian, Mexican, Japanese, Armenian, Christian, Hindu, Buddhist, Muslim, Jewish, etc. You are a human being and that's all!
- All of the so called "special days" are in fact concepts. In reality, there is no such thing as birthdays, anniversaries, national holidays, religious holidays, etc. Even the Calendar is a concept created by the human mind.
- All emotional pain you carry comes from your past or imagined future, both of which are virtual, created by your mind. Certain events have happened, but in reality are not happening any longer, except in your head. It is your mind who keeps them alive in the form of bundles of thoughts and emotions it calls "My past." In the same way, what the mind calls "My future" also consists of bundles of thoughts and emotions, no more. See the true nature of the phantom of "My past and My future." With this logical insight, all of your emotional pains will simply melt away. Then obviously, there is no need to stuff your emotions down with food.
- You judge yourself and everyone else through the filters of "morality, values, traditions, etc." downloaded into your Acquired Self. You were not born with these. Judging yourself and others creates a huge amount of emotional stress. That's why you have such a hard time at work and even at home. Seeing the true nature of morality, ethics, values and traditions will free you from the stress that arises out of *judging*.
- The book of "morality, values and traditions" describes

everyone's role. Naturally, it gives rise to expectations which are the basis of frustrations, annoyances and anger, causing a hard time at work and at home.

- Goals, achievements, material possessions, status, success and failure are all conceptual and in fact are the foundations for greed, ego, frustrations, jealousy, emptiness, loneliness, sadness, unworthiness and bitterness. These emotions are the results of concepts created by the collective human mind and downloaded into your Acquired Self. Entertainment, excessive working, partying and vacationing are simply escapes, and so is *excessive eating*. Look at the root cause of your emotional problems, *the Acquired Self* in you and stop running to escapes.

- "Postponing" is another subtle, but very treacherous trait of the Acquired Self. By telling you to postpone, it keeps itself alive under the radar. However, there is no tomorrow. There is not even the next moment, but only this one! However, the Acquired Self fools you by creating tomorrow. You find yourself saying, "Oh, I understand I have a problem of being overweight, but I will take care of it (tomorrow)." In reality, there is no "tomorrow." Yes, you (or actually your Acquired Self) have a problem. Take care of it right *Now* by freeing yourself from the Acquired Self. Even the phrase "will take care of" has postponement hidden in it.

- Eat *only* to satisfy your hunger. "Food as Fun" is a concept deeply drilled into your Acquired Self by the *Collective Acquired Self of society*. Even "Fun" is a

172

concept, an escape given to you by the Collective Acquired Self of society.

Pay Attention!

With this logical insight, you will be free of your Acquired Self. However, before you know it, it will hijack you again. *Paying attention is crucial.* Pay attention to the tempting thoughts or old eating patterns.

Here are some practical suggestions:

Pay attention to temptations to certain food items that have become part of your Acquired Self such as ice-cream, chocolate, cake, candy, bread, pasta, rice, etc.

Pay attention when you are in the grocery store. Don't buy food items you should not eat.

In order to pay attention, you have to be quiet. That's why you should try not to talk much during your meals. *It is very difficult to pay attention and have a conversation at the same time.* For the same reason, *Do Not* watch TV, read newspapers, magazines or surf the internet while you are eating.

Pay attention to your food. Taste every bite of it.

Be at ease and take your time. Don't be rushed while eating your meal.

Plan ahead for your next meal. Don't get trapped in the usual mind set of "Oh, its' too late to cook anything. Let's order pizza/fast food or find something to heat up in the microwave."

Try to prepare your meals. Pay full attention when you are cooking your meal.

In general, eat only three times a day. Physiologically speaking, grown ups don't need any snacks. Over the age of 50, most people need only two meals a day.

Don't panic if you feel hungry in between meals if you are otherwise healthy, you are not a medicine that can lower your blood sugar or you don't suffer from some medical disease that can cause low blood sugar. Physiologically speaking, you melt away the stored fat in your body when you don't eat at the time of being hungry.

Don't make "losing weight" some kind of mission or goal. This is what the Acquired Self loves to do. When you set up goals of any kind, you are in the grip of your Acquired Self, which will ultimately create stress for you. Stress causes excess release of a stress hormone, cortisol, which causes more weight gain. How counterproductive your Acquired Self is!

Chapter 24

Frustration, Annoyance and Anger

Annoyance, frustration and anger are basically manifestations of the same emotion, only the intensity varies from mild to severe. In its mild form, we call it annoyance and frustration and in a more severe form, we call it anger.

When you are angry, you create huge stress for yourself and everyone else around you. In the grip of anger, your actions are completely illogical, but you don't see it that way. However, someone else can readily see it.

In the heat of anger, you may spew out a flurry of insulting, hateful remarks which can provoke others. They get angry and return even stronger hateful and insulting remarks to you. If the drama of verbal violence continues, it often leads to physical violence.

Later on, when you come to your senses, you may regret what you said or did. That creates even more stress for you. "I am not a good person!" "How could I do that?" "I wish I could take back what I did." "I really didn't mean what I said." In this way, once you come out of your state of *anger*, you get trapped by *shame* and *guilt*.

175

You may promise (*one more time*) to yourself and those around you that you will try to control your anger. You may even get some counseling, attend an anger management seminar or read some books on how to control your anger. You try hard but before you know it, you lose control *again and* become angry. *You say or do* something that you never intended to... And the whole drama keeps repeating itself.

In a less dramatic version, you feel frustrated and annoyed. Often you keep it to yourself. This creates a constant sense of irritability and tension inside you. Sometimes, you verbalize your frustrations in a "civilized" manner. Often, others don't seem to care or may even disagree with your point of view, which upsets you even more. You may promise yourself you're not going to get into any arguments in order to keep peace. In this way, you suppress your anger in order to be civil and polite. However, you feel annoyed and irritated inside... And little things make you more irritated and annoyed.

You may pick up the phone and tell your side of the story to some friendly ears. You may finish half a carton of ice cream or a bag of potato chips or a bottle of wine to get some momentary relief from inner irritation. In fact, you stuff down your frustration and anger with food items... And the drama keeps repeating itself. Actually, you get even more annoyed at your weight gain or your drinking or any other addictive habits. Shame and guilt easily move in. You promise yourself and your loved ones that you will lose weight and be healthy, but keep losing the battle. This frustrates you even more.

176

In some cases, suppression of frustration and anger, especially from childhood, gets so deep that you have no clue where your "comfort eating" comes from. Many people get depressed.

The Root Cause of Anger

If you want to be free of anger, you need to take a close look at it, instead of running away from it. When you use logic and examine what underlies your frustration and anger, you find that it can be a product of one or a combination of the following components of your Acquired Self, the Monster within.

1. Expectations

One of the basic reasons for frustrations and anger is your expectations. You had certain expectations which did not come through and that's why you feel frustrated and angry.

What is the basis of expectations? What do we really mean by expectations? If you look at this question logically, you find that expectations really are a collection of ideas and concepts you acquire during your upbringing. These become part of your Acquired Self, the Monster within.

These concepts revolve around how others should behave towards you and how you should behave towards them. For example, you expect certain kinds of behavior from your

177

spouse, parents, brothers, sisters, friends and colleagues and *vice versa*. In a way, society dictates how each of us should fulfill our role. We can call it the *book of role descriptions,* written by the Society Monster. Each and every person living in a particular society is downloaded with this *book of role descriptions.*

Everyone knows the description of his/her role and also knows the description of the role of others. For example, this book tells you *how a wife should behave, how a husband should behave, how a parent should behave, how a friend should behave, how a child should behave, how a teacher should behave, how a doctor should behave, etc.* Automatically it gives rise to certain expectations.

You expect others to play their part right, by the book. They expect you to play your role right. In other words, everyone is judging everyone else. This is the basis of *Judging.* All morality is derived from this book of role descriptions. If there was no book of role descriptions, there would be no judging; there would be no morality.

Now what happens if someone doesn't play their part right? You get frustrated and at times, angry. It's actually your Acquired Self who feels let down, frustrated and angry, because it is the Acquired Self who builds up expectations. Your Acquired Self believes in all of the ideas contained in the book of role descriptions.

The closer the relationship, the higher the expectations...

178

And more emotional pain if someone does not meet your expectations. This emotional pain manifests as annoyances, frustrations and anger.

Examples:

- *A spouse falling off the ladder of expectations is the most frequent cause of divorce. It goes something like this: In a marriage, as soon as the period of intense sexual romance has cooled, the two monsters show their faces. Now each spouse starts seeing faults in the other person as the person is not living up to expectations. This initially causes annoyance which continues to build up in the memory box and eventually leads to pain and anger. Then one day, there is a big blow up and the marriage ends up in a divorce. Your Monster of expectations is very judgmental and always finds faults in others. Interestingly, it does not see any faults with itself.*

- *Brothers, sisters and close friends get mad and angry if their expectations are not met. Sometimes they end up losing lifelong relationships.*

- *Kids failing to meet the expectations of their parents cause a lot of pain and suffering for their parents as well as themselves. For example, parents expected their son to become a doctor, but the son got poor grades in school. This caused severe headaches and ugly arguments between the son and his parents.*

179

- *Parents expected their daughter to marry someone they thought suitable for her, but she married someone else. Another cause for anger and pain.*

- *A wife expected a gift on her birthday but didn't get anything. The result? Hurt, pain and anger.*

- *A husband expected his wife to be nice to his rowdy buddies, but she called them immature dirt bags which caused a huge argument, pain and anger.*

- *An employee expected a raise, but didn't get one which caused pain and resentment.*

- *A person expected wonderful golden years after retirement, but ended up having cancer which resulted in bitterness and anger in addition to the pain of the news of cancer.*

- *A patient expected a high level of care from his doctor. However, he found out his doctor actually provided poor care. The result? A lot of anger and often a reason for a lawsuit if you live in U.S.A.*

- *In addition to their own personal life, people also build expectations around political and religious figures, movie stars, singers, artists, etc. and get very disappointed and angry if their icon doesn't live up to their expectations. Some even get so angry that they end up killing their icon.*

- *People also create expectations around political, economic and religious systems and get very upset once their expectations are not fulfilled.*

- *People even have expectations about "how long they will live." It is called **life-expectancy**. We feel cheated if someone close to us dies before they were supposed to.*

The Society Monster promises you that you will be rewarded if you follow the rules and punished if you don't. Now what happens if you follow the rules and don't get rewarded and someone who doesn't follow the rules gets rewarded? You get very upset and angry.

For example, you are an honest person suffering economic hardships while some crooked, dishonest liar is rolling in money. "Life isn't fair" you may find yourself saying. You feel very disappointed and angry at life.

True Freedom from Expectations

To be free of annoyance and anger, you need to be free of expectations. You may hear someone advise that "you

181

shouldn't have any expectations." But why not, you ask? Aren't expectations part of normal daily living? How can you even function if there are no expectations?

It is true that most of the world revolves around expectations. Why? Because most of the world is in the grip of the Acquired Self, the conditioned mind. That is one major reason why most people feel frustrated, annoyed and angry. Only if people knew that their True Self has no expectations whatsoever! It's the Acquired Self who builds up all of the expectations and gets hurt when these expectations are not met.

With this realization, you can be free of expectations because they are not part of who you truly are. You can simply let go of the *parasite* that is hurting you. Once you get rid of the root cause, then frustration, annoyance and anger simply do not arise. Then you don't have to practice certain techniques to be free of anger.

2. Self-righteousness

Another common reason for anger and frustration is self-righteousness.

What is self-righteousness? In simple terms, it means "I am right." It also implies that "you are wrong." This is the root cause of all disagreements, disputes, arguments, quarrels, fights, lawsuits, battles and wars, all of which obviously create a huge amount of anger.

With few exceptions, everyone suffers from self-righteousness. Interestingly, people don't like to be called self-righteous because it's considered a bad quality. They don't think they are self-righteous, but they readily see it in others. They simply judge others to be self-righteous and don't go any deeper. Actually, they believe they are *right* that someone else is self-righteous. Interesting, isn't it?

Self-righteousness is an extremely common affliction and one of the reasons for all human conflicts. If we want to understand human conflicts, it makes sense to look at self-righteousness more deeply.

What is the Basis of Self-Righteousness?

Why do we believe that we are right and others are wrong? For example, for the same event, different people will have different opinions. Each one believes that he is right and others are wrong. The event is the same, but its interpretations are very different. Obviously, the problem lies in the interpretations. Now who is it that is doing the interpretation? It's your Acquired Self, isn't it? What is the Acquired Self? It's knowledge, concepts, ideas and stories about your own experiences, others experiences and collective human experiences, etc. Basically it consists of tons and tons of information and associated emotions residing inside you which you acquire as you grow up.

Typically when a person looks at an event, he interprets that event against the background of the already stored information and emotions in his Acquired Self. Obviously, this stored information and emotions varies from person to person. Therefore, interpretation of the same event varies from person to person. With few exceptions, it is the Acquired Self who interprets events. A majority of people are in the grip of their Acquired Selves. They completely identify with their Acquired Self. That's who they believe they are! Therefore, they strongly believe that their interpretation of the event is *right*.

If we look deeper at the composition of a person's Acquired Self, we find that the *book of role descriptions* is an important part of it. This book, as we observed earlier, describes how a person *should* and *should not* behave in a given society. In addition to creating expectations, it also provides a background against which everyone keeps judging others behavior. It tells you and everyone else "what is *right* and what is *wrong*"; "what is *virtue* and what is *evil*." This is the basis of *morality*.

These are basically concepts given to you by your Society Monster. Using these concepts, everyone judges others and society judges everyone living in it. Now, if you are in the total grip of your Acquired Self, you believe these concepts to be the *truth*. You honestly believe that you are *right,* because you believe in certain concepts and those who don't believe in those concepts are *wrong*. Which of course is *self-righteousness*.

184

In the grip of self-righteousness, you are constantly annoyed and at times angry at those who do not believe in the same concepts as you do. Your Acquired Self believes that you are right and others are wrong.

In addition to the *book of role descriptions*, your Society Monster also downloads into your Acquired Monster, many other concepts. For example, it gives you the concepts about "your rights," "human rights" and "animal rights." All of these concepts become part of your Acquired Self and give you more ammunition to be *right*. These concepts strengthen your self-righteousness.

When you are in the grip of your Acquired Self, theses concepts become your *beliefs*. When others don't follow what you believe in, you get frustrated and angry.

In addition, your Society Monster downloads into your Acquired Self the knowledge of history, which primarily is an interpretation of certain events by the Acquired Self of the historian-writer. That is the reason why there are so many different interpretations of the same events and of course, every historian believes he is right. The historian's interpretation of events becomes part of your Acquired Self and you believe them to be absolutely true (although the event may have happened before you and the historian were even born). Different Acquired Selves with different versions of the same historic event or historic figure then get into heated arguments and get angry at each other.

185

With this background, your Acquired Self also judges current political events. Usually, it is some so called expert who does it for you, on a TV show, in a newspaper or in a book. Acquired Selves with different versions of history interpret current events differently and each one believes he is right. With this background, people get into heated arguments and get mad and angry at each other.

It is interesting to note that in a given society, there are collective concepts about what is right and what is wrong. This creates a *collective self-righteousness*, which gets reinforced constantly by the news-media in that society. *What is right in one society may be wrong in another society.* This creates conflict between various societies. That's why people living in one society get angry at another society. This is the basis of *collective conflict, anger and violence* between various nations.

Then, within a given society, there are various concepts about what is right and what is wrong, depending upon various social, political and religious groups in that society. This creates conflict, anger and violence between various groups within a society.

Then within a group, there are various concepts about what is right and what is wrong. Therefore, within the same group, people get angry and fight among each other. Even within a family, there are various concepts about what is right and what is wrong. It leads to conflict, anger and violence (usually verbal but sometimes even physical) between various members of the same family. For example, you may be a strong believer of animal rights and your husband may not agree with you. This could lead to a serious argument and verbal conflict.

Then, within an individual, there are conflicting concepts what is right and what is wrong. There is one code of ethics for the work place and another one for home, one code of ethics for friends and another one for enemies, one standard for yourself and another one for everyone else.

It all boils down to "I, My, Me, Mine" Syndrome. Based on the concepts attached to "I, My, Me, Mine," you judge everyone else out there as either your friend or enemy. That's how you perceive other people - as either your friends or your enemies: at home, in your neighborhood, at your work place, in your social, political or religious group, in your country and in the world. You stay annoyed and angry at your enemies, which often leads to violence, verbal as well as physical.

True Freedom from Self-Righteousness.

If you want to be free of self-righteousness, you need to first admit that you are suffering from self-righteousness. And here is the biggest dilemma - when you strongly believe you are *right*, how can you ever admit that you are *not right*? That's why most people continue to suffer from self-righteousness and its consequences of anger and even hate.

If you are willing to entertain the idea that you may not

187

be right, then there is a chance that you may be free of the prison of self-righteousness. If you are willing to use logic (not intellectual rationalization, which is simply a product of acquired knowledge), then you will see the root cause of self-righteousness, as we observed earlier in the chapter.

Once you have a logical insight into the mechanics of self-righteousness, you will happily get out of the prison of self-righteousness. With that, anger automatically dies out.

3. Fear

Another reason why people get angry is their deep seated fear, but they usually don't know it. Usually, the more short tempered a person is on the surface, the more fearful he is inside. Expressing anger outwardly is a gesture of extreme insecurity inside. People try to scare others with their anger while they are fearful themselves. How ironic!

Most people don't even realize that their "bursts of anger" are actually arising out of a volcano of fear and insecurity.

If you are serious about getting to the bottom of the root causes of your anger, you have to examine yourself sincerely. Quite likely, you will find that you feel quite fearful and insecure inside.

The Root Cause of Fear

Fear actually arises from the memory of a bad event, which has become part of your Acquired Self. Your Acquired Self learns from this bad event and says "this should never happen to me again". However, then comes another thought - "what if" and that creates a huge amount of fear. In this way, your Acquired Self becomes quite insecure. Hence, it seeks security. In the pursuit of security, it wants to control the behavior of others. However, when it can't control others, it gets very angry. Even a trigger in the form of a news article or a story that reminds the Acquired Self that it cannot control others, can throw it into a rage.

Examples:

A father sees a program about teenagers frequently using illegal drugs and how it adversely affects their life. His Acquired Self absorbs this story and makes it part of itself, as if this was his own experience. Then comes another thought - "this should never happen to my son." He tells his son not to mix with certain kinds of people at school. "In this way I should be able to prevent my son from taking drugs." Then one day he sees his son with a shady character which triggers "what if my son is on drugs" and that thought triggers a huge amount of fear in him. Seeing that he has no control over his son's behavior makes him very insecure inside. However, outwardly, he will have an outburst of anger at his son.

Collectively, groups of people holding onto their collective past get fearful with thoughts of "what if it happens again." Hence, they want to secure their future by controlling the behavior of others. Any reminder that they can't control the behavior of others creates a wave of fear, which can express as anger and can lead to violence against another group of people.

True Freedom from Fear

People often try to conquer their fear by one technique or another. It may work temporarily but sooner or later, they are back in the grip of their fear.

Only when you know the root cause of fear, you can be free of it once and for all. Then, there is no need to learn various techniques to control your fear.

As we observed, fear arises from some bad memory in the past and the mind generating more thoughts in its effort to learn from it and prevent similar bad things from happening again. You must realize that a "bad event" is not happening at this moment any longer. It happened, yes, but is not happening at this moment. It is being kept alive only through the activity of your mind. Otherwise, in reality, it is dead and gone. This realization will free you completely from fear.

Because the memory of a bad event does not control your mind any more, there is no need to think this may happen again and obviously, then your mind does not create more thoughts on how to prevent it. That's how the whole infrastructure of anger simply crumbles and you get the ultimate freedom from fear.

4. Insults

Another reason why people get angry is *insults.* Obviously, you get angry when someone insults you. You *may or may not* express your anger.

Many people fight back by returning insulting remarks or gestures. Also, there are those who pretend to be polite and civilized on the surface, while fuming with anger underneath. Later, they often express their anger while talking to their spouse or friends. Some even suppress anger so deeply that on the surface, they manage to remain polite and civilized all the time. They may even try to fake a smile, but deep inside, they feel irritated and don't even know why they feel that way!

What is the Basis of Insults?

Is it possible for you to never be insulted? I'm not talking about suppressing your anger and pretending that you are not insulted, but in reality - to not actually feel insulted at all when someone insults you.

In order to be truly free of insults, you first need to figure out, "who is it inside you who gets insulted in the first place."

Use logic and you will find that it's your Acquired Self who gets insulted. The True Self never gets insulted. Why do I say that? Because a newborn baby never gets insulted. You can try to insult a baby by saying whatever you want, but the baby will not be insulted. In the same way, imagine some one trying to insult you in a language or through gestures that you don't understand. Obviously, you will not be insulted. Therefore, we can conclude that for the insult to occur, one has to understand the *concepts* attached to those words and gestures. Otherwise, they have no power.

Where do you learn the words and gestures and all of the concepts attached to them? You are not born with them. You obviously learn them as you grow up in a certain society. That's why it is logical to conclude it's your Acquired Self who gets insulted.

With every word, there is a concept attached. For example, the word STUPID has a whole concept of unintelligence, inadequacy and worthlessness attached to it. When your developing monster learns this word, it stores all the negative concepts attached to the word. When someone calls you by that word, the negative concept attached to that word is activated and negative thoughts trigger negative emotions. You feel unintelligent, worthless, inadequate and angry. *You didn't deserve it. How dare someone say that to you.* Actually, your monster's sense of self-esteem is threatened. Therefore, your monster fights back verbally or even physically in order to secure its existence, its self-esteem.

192

The insulting words are created by the Society Monster for the individual monsters to fight with each other, aren't they?

Society's Collective Acquired Self downloads the concept of "*insult and respect*" into your Acquired Self. When others respect you, your Acquired Self feels validated and when others insult you, your Acquired Self feels humiliated. In other words, your Acquired Self is constantly reacting to how others treat it. Your Acquired Self wants to be respected and not be insulted. Obviously, it has no control over others' behavior, but it doesn't know this basic fact. It just keep searching for respect and running away from insult. It is especially true if at an early age you were insulted (teased) a lot. Your Acquired Self felt humiliated and all of those painful experiences become part of your Acquired Self. Then, your Acquired Self found a way (academics, sports, arts, etc.) for others to start respecting you. Your Acquired Self finally got the praise and validation it was so hungry for. Naturally, your Acquired Self works hard on this track and usually ends up being quite accomplished and successful in that field. With each step of success, it gets more respect, praise and validation and it loves it all. *The more it gets attached to respect, the more it resents the idea of insult.* Then, a trivial teasing remark can upset your Acquired Self for days. You may even burst into anger in a social situation where you didn't get enough respect, which you perceive as an insult.

True Freedom from Insults

Often, others (usually those who care about you) can see your over-reactions and suggest anger management. So you try the usual venues society offers such as counseling, books, seminars, etc., but nothing really works for you. Sooner or later, you again explode in a rage or you sizzle inside over some insulting remark someone made days ago. Often, you get even more annoyed, even ashamed, that you are holding grudges, because you know that's a bad thing. Most people stay trapped in the prison of insults for the rest of their life.

Is it possible to be free of insults? The answer is yes, but only when you get to the root of the problem. When you realize that it is your Acquired Self that gets insulted, you can be free of insults by freeing yourself from your Acquired Self. Then, you realize that it is your Acquired Self who is holding onto painful memories when it felt insulted. Those painful experiences are not happening in the present moment, but only happening in your head. This simple realization can free you of the huge load of painful memories. You also realize that you don't have to keep proving your worth and being praised by others. The need for praise simply vanishes. Then, you don't react to remarks of praise or insult. People can say whatever they want: it does not make you elated or angry.

Free of your Acquired Self, you live in joy, peace and bliss that is never threatened.

Once you fully realize the mechanics of insulting words, you'll laugh (in your head) when someone uses an insulting remark, won't you? Because you will see that the other person's Acquired Self is doing what it has been conditioned to do and in reality, it does not mean a thing. Then there is no need to fight back.

It is quite likely that even with all this wisdom, your Acquired Self will get engaged and fight back next time you're insulted. However, minutes or even hours later, you may be able to see the "real mechanics of insult."

The moment you see insult in its true colors, you'll be free of it, instead of fuming for days. Next time, in the middle of an insult, you may see your own Acquired Self getting engaged and trying to fight back. Simply seeing your monster in action will free you of its tight hold on you. You may actually burst into laughter. In this way, no one will be able to insult you. *People may try to insult you, but you won't get insulted.*

Q: I can't accept the fact that there are so many bad people in the world. How can I not be angry?

A: If you stay angry because there are so many bad people in the world, you are simply hurting yourself. It doesn't solve any problem, does it? Some people get so angry they may individually or collectively resort to violence, but it still doesn't solve the problem. *Violence begets more violence.*

195

Instead of being angry, isn't it worthwhile to examine why people act in a bad way? If you truly want to understand why some people have bad behavior, you have to leave the usual explanations for bad behavior behind and take a fresh look using your own logic, not what you have been told.

If you use logic, then you will find that the root cause of all bad behavior is in fact, the individual Acquired Self, as well as the Collective Acquired Self. Look deeply and you will find that the underlying cause for bad behavior is greed, ego, selfishness, self-righteousness, anger, hate, jealousy or fear. All of these are products of the Acquired Self. Therefore, the world cannot be free of bad behavior as long as it is in the grip of the Acquired Self. When you are in the grip of the Acquired Self, you see faults with everyone except yourself. The fact is that everyone who is in the grip of the Acquired Self ends up with so called bad behavior whether he admits it or not.

You cannot force people to get rid of their Acquired Self. This kind of behavior is actually a desire to control others' behavior and it comes out of your own Acquired Self and is very tempting. Once you see that bad human behavior arises out of selfishness, greed, ego, insecurity, desire to control others, self-righteousness, anger, hate, bitterness and fear, you get enlightened. However, often it lasts for only a brief period.

Before you know it, self-righteousness and ego creep back in without you being aware of it. Then, you start to think that

196

you're *right* and the entire world is *wrong* and you become angry at the whole world... or you get the urge to awaken the entire world from their deep psychological sleep.

Just remember, whenever you think you're right and others are wrong, you are in the grip of your self-righteousness. When you think you have to accomplish some heroic mission, you are in the grip of your ego.

All you should be concerned with is to free yourself from your *own* Acquired Self and that's it. You change the world inside you, and that's all. The outside world is a reflection of the world inside you.

Unfortunately, most people blame others for all the problems in the world and want to change others' behaviors except their own. This is the strategy of the Acquired Self. It does not work, but helps to perpetuate and even worsen bad behavior.

It doesn't mean that you can't stop someone who, for example, is trying to rob you. You will automatically do whatever needs to be done when a *real* situation arises. What you need to do is to free yourself from all hypothetical situations, stories and concepts that your conditioned mind creates for you, which, of course, it does with the help of the Society Monster in the form of news media, books, the internet, etc.

Chapter 25

Grievances, Hate and Revenge

Grievances and *hate* are very deep seated emotions. Revenge is an action arising out of *grievances* and *hate*. Not only individuals harbor hate, but groups of people, societies and nations also harbor *hate* and *grievances*.

While *hate* creates a constant burning and irritation inside you, *revenge* arising out of this hate inflicts tremendous sufferings on other human beings. However, you don't look at them as human beings. The fire of *hate* makes you blind. You look at others as your enemies who must be defeated, destroyed and annihilated. Your actions obviously reinforce *hate* in others, who try to inflict sufferings on you as much as they can and the *"ping - pong of violence"* continues.

Deep down, you and your enemies are also afraid of each other. The *desire* to dominate and annihilate each other becomes more and more intense. Therefore, you and your enemies are constantly at work developing new tricks, new strategies, new technologies and new weapons to dominate, defeat and annihilate each other. This is the basis of the never ending cycle of violence. This is also the basis of the never ending cycle of wars.

Sooner or later, you get tired of the huge stress that *hate* and *grievances* creates for you and others. You want to find some answers, so you turn to your Society Monster. What does it tell you? *"Hate, grievances and revenge are not good. You should be loving and peaceful. You should be non-violent."* That sounds wonderful, but in the next breath it also advises you *"to fight and defeat your enemies."* In essence, what the Society Monster tells you is to pick and choose. *"Be peaceful and loving towards your friends, but be hateful and vengeful towards your enemies."*

Well, as we all know, this philosophy does not work at all. That's why there is so much hate, revenge and violence inside you, all around you and in the world despite all sorts of religious, social and political preaching promoting non-violence, peace and love.

Is It Possible to be Free of Hate, Grievances and Revenge?

Is it possible to be rid of hate, grievances and revenge? Society will tell you that it is not possible. It may even tell you that hate is part of "human nature." *"You fight for your survival. Therefore fighting is human nature,"* your Society Monster may explain. These explanations become part of your Acquired Self, which therefore, justify hate and violence.

Is it possible for you to be free of hate and revenge? If you earnestly try to find the answer for yourself, you need to set aside all explanations you have been given. Only then, you can look at the problem with *logic*. Like a true scientist, you have to be

200

free of all preconceived notions to investigate a problem.

What is the Root Cause of Hate and Grievances?

In order to cure hate, you need to diagnose its root cause, right? What is the root cause of hate and grievances? Why do you hate someone? Isn't it because you believe someone is your *enemy*? Why do you believe that someone is your enemy? Because someone did something bad to you in the *past* or you've been told that some one or some group did something bad to your ancestors in the *past*.

"My" (or Our) enemy and *"My" (or Our) past* are clearly the root cause of hate and grievances.

"My" Enemy

Let us take a closer look at "My" enemy." Who is it that's really talking? It's your Acquired Self, isn't it? "I, My, Me, Mine" Syndrome, as we observed earlier, is at the *core* of your Acquired Self. It divides you from every one else on the planet. Then, you perceive yourself as "I" and everyone else as "others." You look at the world through the window of the concepts drilled into your Acquired Self such as religious, social and political ideas. Those who have ideas *similar* to the ideas in your Acquired Self become your friends and those with *opposing* ideas become your enemies. This is the basis of "My" (or Our) enemies.

"My" Past

Now let's take a look at "My" (or Our) past. What is the past? Your Acquired Self takes a mental picture of every event, and judges it good or bad based upon the *book of role descriptions* already downloaded. Judging triggers an emotion and then the whole bundle of "event, judgment and emotion get stored in memory. That's how your mind creates your past. Later, it keeps visiting the stored events (memories) over and over again.

Let's say, you had an event that your Acquired Self judged to be a *defeat* due to *unfairness* and stored it as a bad memory. Each time your mind visits this *unfair event of defeat*, you feel a wave of rage rising inside you. Unfairness triggers *bitterness, hate and rage* which are quite deep seated. Now, you want to defeat the person who defeated you in the past and caused you so much stress. You want to get even and cause him pain and suffering. Only this time around, you will use any means. You will even be unfair. *"So what? I was a victim of unfairness once,"* you rationalize. Your Society Monster validates these thoughts. *"There is no fairness in war. Life is unfair."*

In addition to your personal past, your Society Monster has created its own collective past and it is downloaded into your Acquired Self as part of your upbringing. This is the basis of *collective grievances and bitterness* against a certain historic figure or a group of people. Perpetuation of bitterness and grievances often leads to violence which creates more bad

202

memories and feeds more bitterness and grievances. *That's how hate thrives.*

In the grip of your hate and grievances, you (and collectively your group) become so irrational that you may inflict pain and suffering on people who have nothing to do with your past. It is usually people with less power, such as your employees, children, wife and underprivileged people. You just want to *"give it to some one."*

True Freedom from Hate, Grievances and Revenge

Now for a moment consider that you are free of "I, My, Me, Mine" Syndrome and free of the personal as well as the collective past. Do you have any hate or grievances left? The answer obviously is No! When you are free of hate and grievances, you are automatically free of the desire to avenge.

Now the big question is how do you get freedom from the "I, My, Me, Mine" Syndrome? Use logic and you realize you were *not* born with this. It was given to you by your Society Monster.

How do you get freedom from your personal and collective past? Use logic and you realize that the past only exists in your head. Of course, it was real when it happened, but now it is a phantom - unreal because it is not happening in the Now.

Once free of the "I, My, Me, Mine" Syndrome and free of the past, you will not have any hate or grievances. Then obviously, you won't have any enemies. Automatically, there is no need to take revenge. That's how violence ends spontaneously.

Q: Aren't hate and violence human nature?

A: Hate and violence are the nature of the Acquired Self. If you totally identify with your Acquired Self and that's who you think you are, then you will believe that hate and violence are human nature. The Society Monster reinforces this concept into your Acquired Self. *"Everyone else believes in it. I saw experts on TV believing in it, so it must be true,"* says your Acquired Self.

Only when you are free of your Acquired Self, can you clearly see that hate, grievances and violence are the product of the Acquired Self.

If you want to see true human nature, observe newborn babies. They are not hateful or violent, are they? To the contrary, they are so peaceful, loving and joyful. They don't judge anyone on the basis of color, creed, religion or nationality. They have no friends and no enemies. They don't hold hate or grievances because they are devoid of the "Acquired Self."

Q: I hate violence. I believe in non-violence, peace and love. I have joined groups who promote these wonderful ideas. Isn't that great?

A: Violence is the result of hate. When you say," I <u>hate</u> violence," aren't you adding fuel to the fire? Don't you have to look at the hate itself? What's the root cause of hate? Once you figure that out, then you can be free of violence without *hating* violence.

As we observed earlier, hate is the product of the Acquired Self. Certain ideas such as non-violence and world peace seem noble and wonderful. *However, any idea or concept is ultimately part of the Acquired Self.* As long as people are in the grip of their Acquired Selves, psychologically speaking, they are divided from each other. **As long as there is division, there will be conflict.** It is so logical! Conflict is the foundation of violence and peace cannot be when there is violence. Therefore, there cannot be real peace as long as people are in the grip of their Acquired Selves.

Concepts divide human beings from each other. That is the basis of conflict and violence. Any concept, however wonderful and noble, cannot (and obviously has not) free humans from conflict and violence.

Q: Isn't "survival of the fittest" the basis of our evolution? Therefore, we should be strong in order to survive.

A: What Darwin proposed as the basis of evolution was "the process of natural selection," which later, the laymen press changed into "survival of the fittest." In fact, *survival of the most adaptable* is a more accurate interpretation of "the process of natural selection." Fittest is not the most accurate interpretation because it somehow points towards being powerful and strong. As we know, some of the most powerful animals, such as dinosaurs, are extinct now and some of the weakest animals, such as ants and butterflies, have survived.

When we talk survival in terms of evolution, we talk of the real survival of a species. When people talk of survival of the fittest, they give it as an excuse for wars and killing other human beings. Obviously, they are not talking about the survival of the collective human race. They are talking of survival of those humans who have similar ideas and concepts as their own. They are talking about survival of their own Collective Acquired Selves, aren't they?

Q: Violence is part of nature. You see it when an animal kills another animal. So why are people so against violence these days?

A: You are confusing *killing* with *violence*. To you, killing means violence. In nature, when an animal kills another animal, it is either hungry or defending itself or its babies from another animal. However, when people kill each other, they don't do it because they are hungry or actually threatened. Humans often kill each other because they are *psychologically* threatened, although there is often no real threat to their existence as humans. They wage

206

wars to defend their religious, nationalistic or political ideologies. They often kill others, not because they are hungry, but to have more land, more wealth, more power, etc.

Now when an animal kills another animal, it is not defending its religious or political beliefs. However, looking through the filters of your Acquired Self, you call it violence and therefore, justify violence that people carry out against each other.

The Acquired Self is very cunning, clever and treacherous. It lures you with very noble, wonderful, and intellectually appealing ideas. However, you can cut through its disguise with logic, your ultimate intelligence.

Q: I am trying hard to be non-violent, peaceful and loving. Can you suggest some techniques?

A: Violence and hate are the products of the Acquired Self. In contrast, your True Self, the one you are born with, is *non-violent, loving* and *peaceful.* This is your true nature and that is the true nature of every other human being as well. As you can see, you already have this wonderful human being sitting inside you. The source of love, peace and nonviolence is inside you - your True Self. But it gets eclipsed by your Acquired Self. Lost in the Acquired Self, you search for something out there that already resides inside you. You search for more concepts and ideas to be non-violent, peaceful and loving. *All concepts are part of the Acquired Self.* Therefore, the more you search for nonviolence, peace and love, the more you get in the grip of your Acquired Self and the farther you get from your True Self. Can you understand how counterproductive your search for nonviolence, love and peace is?

So stop searching for nonviolence, love and peace. All you need to do is be free of your Acquired Self and let your True Self *illuminate* you. The True Self is *real*, not a concept. Therefore, you can only experience it, feel it, be it. You cannot describe it. Why? Because words themselves are products of the Collective Acquired Self. *Words create concepts and the True Self is not a concept.*

Q: *I see so much violence and suffering in the world. I want to change the world. I believe love can change the world. And that is my mission: to change the world with love.*

A: People have been trying to change the world with a variety of wonderful ideas including the idea of love. However, the reality is something like this: Over the last 5000 years or so of known human history, people have not changed a bit, in psychological terms. We have made great progress in terms of technology but psychologically speaking, we humans are as violent, hateful, revengeful, jealous and fearful as we ever were. Why?

Before you answer, please be still for a moment. Take a fresh look at the root cause of violence and suffering before you embark on the mission to cure this widespread ailment of human beings.

As we observed earlier, the root cause of *violence* is *conflict*, which results from human beings divided into groups because of concepts. In other words, attachment to concepts divides human beings from each other which leads to conflict and violence.

To put it in another way, it is the Acquired Self that separates human from each other. As long as humans are separated from each other, there will be conflict and violence. Instead of looking at the root cause of violence and human suffering, the Acquired Self distracts you by conveniently providing you with more concepts such as *love, peace and nonviolence*. By creating this distraction, the Acquired Self skillfully avoids detection and continues to thrive.

Now perhaps, you understand why humans have not changed in their psychological behavior. As a byproduct of evolution and civilization, the human mind created the Acquired Self in every individual. In the grip of the Acquired Self, humans remain divided and create a huge amount of suffering for each other. Then, they try to find a solution for these sufferings through the filters of their own Acquired Self. Hence, everyone wants to change the world according to his/her own wishes and concepts. Deep down, everyone wants to control the world by changing it according to their own likes and dislikes, according to their own ideas and concepts. In doing so, we create more conflicts, more violence and more suffering.

Let me clarify the term Love. As we observed earlier in the book, when we use the word love, we are talking of the concept attached to this word. The *concept of love is a creation of the human mind.* This love easily changes into hate when things are not the way they are supposed to be, according to the concept of love.

In contrast, there is True Love, which is not a concept and therefore cannot be described. It can only be felt but not described.

Change the World!

So, "You" want to change the world
But so do "I"
"You" want to change the world
And
"I" want to change the world
But
If there is no "You"
And there is no "Me"
Then there is no need,
to change the world.

Sarfraz Zaidi

Chapter 26

Hypocrisy

We call someone a hypocrite if they pretend to be nice, virtuous and pious, but in fact, they are *not*. A person deceives when they are being hypocritical.

It is interesting to note that a hypocritical person does not see himself as a hypocrite, although others may clearly see it. Why? Because the word hypocrite carries a negative connotation. These people consider themselves to be polite, nice and diplomatic - much better words than hypocritical.

When we call a person hypocritical, aren't we passing judgment against her? It makes you somehow feel like a better person, doesn't it? "Oh, she's a hypocrite." What you really imply is: "I'm a better person than her because she is deceitful and I'm not." Often, people call someone a hypocrite when that person is not present, but pretend to be nice to them on their face. Isn't that hypocrisy as well? With few exceptions, most people are hypocritical.

What is the Root Cause of Hypocrisy?

In order to be free of hypocrisy, we need to look deeper

211

at it instead of running away from it. First, we have to admit that we are hypocritical. Only then, can we go deeper.

Who is it inside of you who *pretends* to be nice, polite and virtuous? It's your Acquired Self, isn't it? What is nice, polite and virtuous? Concepts, right? Do newborn babies pretend to be polite, nice and virtuous? Obviously *not*. The concepts of nice, polite and virtuous get downloaded into your Acquired Self, along with a number of other concepts as you grow up in society. Greed, selfishness, anger, hate, bitterness, revenge, bias, prejudice, violence, addiction, self-righteousness, fear and jealousy are some of the products of these concepts. In other words, society trains your Acquired Self to be greedy, selfish, hateful, revengeful and biased. At the same time, it teaches your Acquired Self to *be* polite, nice and virtuous. And then it labels this behavior as *hypocrisy*. Interesting, isn't it?

True Freedom from Hypocrisy

Once you fully understand the root cause of hypocrisy, will you still be hypocritical? Obviously *not*. Once you realize you are not your Acquired Self, you are free of the concept of "nice, polite and virtuous." At the same time, you also get freedom from greed, selfishness, anger, hate, revenge, jealousy, fear, bias and prejudice. Then, you become a truly nice, kind and virtuous person *without trying* to be one. This is how hypocrisy automatically ends.

212

Chapter 27

Guilt and Self Criticism

A large number of people carry the heavy burden of *guilt*. Often, they don't even talk about it and suffer in isolation. Most think they can't do anything about it and they have to live with it for the rest of their life.

Some may decide to seek help, but often nothing really works and they continue to suffer. Sometimes, other people may even try to take advantage by threatening them with the punishment of guilt.

What is the Root Cause of Guilt?

If you want to be free of guilt, you obviously need to get to the root of the diagnosis: What really causes guilt? Why does someone feel guilty?

If you use logic, you realize guilt comes from the memory of some event with a bad outcome and you feel that you could have prevented it from happening. In this way, you feel responsible for the event.

Now let's find out who is it that feels guilty. It's your Acquired Self, isn't it? Some event occurred that is not happening

213

any longer, but is still very much alive in your head. Your mind took a mental picture of the event, judged it to be bad based upon the information stored in your mind and that triggered a bad emotion. Then, the entire bundle of the mental picture, the attached story and the associated emotion got stored in your memory box. It's a crafty work of your mind, isn't it? In reality, the event is long dead and gone, but in your mind, it remains alive. Why? Because your mind has conveniently preserved it to torture you for the rest of your life. Interesting how the mind works!

Why does the mind take mental pictures and judge them to be good and bad and then preserve them as memory? Because, that's exactly how the *conditioned* mind works.

In the real world, events happen continuously, with each event having a beginning and ending, the cycle of birth and death, one of the fundamental laws of nature. The conditioned human mind however, works against this law of nature. It is conditioned to dislike death. It does not want anything to die. Therefore, it creates memories of events and in this way, keeps them alive in the head and gives them virtual life.

Why does the conditioned human mind judge events as good or bad? Because, it is conditioned to do so. As a part of conditioning, your mind gets downloaded with the book of "role descriptions." For example, it tells you how a good husband should behave, how a good wife should behave, how a good parent, a good child, a good neighbor should behave. These are basically concepts that society has created for you to live in it.

214

They obviously have their place, their functional value. However, you (and everyone else) believe in them as Truth. You don't look at them for what they really are: concepts.

Now what happens if you are unable to behave according to this book of role descriptions? You will obviously judge yourself to be a bad husband, wife, parent or child. This is the basis of *self-criticism and guilt.*

True Freedom from Guilt and Self-Criticism

Perhaps now you understand, you can never be free of guilt and self-criticism as long as you are in the grip of your Acquired Self, because your Acquired Self (which is your conditioned mind) is the root cause of your guilt and self-criticism.

Once you clearly see the whole mechanics of guilt and self-criticism, you can be free of it. Simply seeing with clarity is enough.

Caution:

Please don't start to rebel against the rules of your society. These rules are made by society as a means for the society to function. As long as you live in a society, you need to obey its rules, which are basically concepts. Problem arises when you start to believe in these concepts as something more than concepts. Then, you *seriously* start to judge others and yourself. In this way, you create a heavy burden of anger and guilt. Simply see these concepts as concepts created by society. That's all!

Chapter 28

Embarrassment and Shame

As you grow up, you pick up a lot of ideas along the way including a lot of *manners* from your parents, school, news media, movies, etc. That's how you acquire your Acquired Self.

What is the Basis of Embarrassment and Shame?

In other words, that's how your mind gets conditioned by society, which tells you what's right and what's wrong; what's desirable and what's not; what's acceptable and what's not.

Equipped with this information, your Acquired Self judges others all the time and knows that others are judging it as well. If you or someone close to you, say your child, falls below the standards set by society, your Acquired Self feels embarrassed, which is a feeling of uneasiness, shame and humiliation.

Examples:

- Your ten year old daughter does not listen to you in front of your friends. You feel ashamed of her behavior, because you *failed* to teach her the manners of "respecting your elders."

217

- When your husband starts talking loud after a couple of drinks, you feel embarrassed and ashamed of his behavior because you feel as if you married a *loser*.

- You go to a party without having proper attire. You feel embarrassed, because deep down, you feel *ignorant* or *poor*.

- You go to a restaurant or a club by yourself and feel uneasy, thinking that others may judge you to be a *loser* with no friends.

- You arrive late to a party because traffic was horrible. You feel embarrassed and apologetic because you think others might judge you to be a *rude* person.

- In a conversation, because you did not know some historic fact, you feel embarrassed because others may think you are an *ignorant* person.

Your Acquired Self wants to be *accepted* by other members of the clan. The desire to be part of the clan is to cover up a deep rooted sense of insecurity. The larger the insecurity, the more clinging to the manners and standards of the clan. You see it in its extreme form in so called "high society" country clubs, where you are judged by if *you wore the proper tie and shoes with your suit or if you used the right utensils during dinner.*

Deeply caught up in your Acquired Self, you feel extremely sensitive to anything less than perfect (according to the club rules) and you get easily embarrassed.

These moments of embarrassment and humiliation get stored in your memory box and create a huge amount of shame and unworthiness. These memories then generate further thoughts that this embarrassment should not happen in the future. That's why you develop a *fear* of embarrassment as well.

True Freedom from Embarrassment and Shame

If only people knew the root cause of embarrassment and shame, they could be free of it in a moment. The simple realization that embarrassment and shame is not part of your True Self, but part of your Acquired Self, is very liberating. Then you can truly let go of it. Just imagine the relief you get just knowing that all of the embarrassment and shame you harbor is not the true you, but all of it was shoved down your throat in the name of *manners* and *culture*. That's how you get freedom from the life-long learned behavior which causes you embarrassment and shame.

219

Chapter 29

Fear

What is fear? It is an unpleasant emotion, isn't it? In its mild form, it manifests itself as a sense of *uneasiness* and *nervousness*. In its moderate form, it manifests as *insomnia* and *anxiety* and in its severe form, it manifests as *panic attacks* and *phobias*. With few exceptions, everyone suffers from one or more of the various manifestations of fear.

Most people aren't even aware of the connection between fear and their "uneasiness, nervousness, insomnia, anxiety, panic attacks and phobias."

What is the Root Cause of Fear?

What are you afraid of? Most people reply "I am fearful because of *this* and *that*." However, if you want to know the root cause of fear, you need to use logic. Then you realize that fear actually comes from your own mind, not from *things* out there.

Fear is a psychological state created by your own *conditioned* mind. For example, you may become afraid and panicky just by thinking:

- *What if I lose my job?*

221

- *What if lose my wife?*
- *What if I lose my business?*
- *What if I lose my health?*
- *What if I lose my life?*
- *What if I miss my flight?*
- *What if people make fun of me again?*
- *What if I get stuck in the elevator?*
- *What if I can't find a job?*
- *What if I can't find a boyfriend?*
- *What if I don't pass the exam?*
- *What if I develop cancer?*
- *What if I lose my autonomy?*

If you pay attention, you realize that there are *two* essential components in the thought process that creates fear.

1. "I, Me, My, Mine"
2. A hypothetical situation, which "I" perceives as a threat.

Let's take a closer look at the "I." It's your Acquired Self, isn't it? Fear is created by your Acquired Self to protect itself. When you identify with your Acquired Self, obviously you feel all of this fear. In the grip of your Acquired Self, you will continue to stay fearful.

Your Acquired Self basically consists of concepts, information, experiences and their associated emotions. Now let's see how your Acquired Self creates fear for itself.

The virtual "I" contains several concepts such as concept of wealth, beauty, possessions, profession, family, health, nationality, religion, culture etc. In order to survive, "I" has to protect these concepts. Any thought that it may *lose* any of its components obviously creates a virtual threat and resultant fear for the "I", your Acquired Self. For example, if "I" believe in the concept of beauty, any thought of losing beauty will create a lot of fear for the "I." In the same way, if someone's Acquired Self is heavily invested in being a lawyer, doctor or engineer (or any other profession), any thought of losing its license will create a lot of fear for the "I" of that person.

Your Acquired Self does not want to ever lose anything or anyone that is "Mine." That's why it looks for security, which in reality does not exist. The more possessions you have as "Mine," the more you fear losing them and the more you try to protect them. For example, you may end up living in a gated community to protect your belongings. You may become a frequent visitor to a plastic surgeon to preserve your looks. One day you may notice you're losing your hair, which may trigger huge fear. I have seen patients wanting to be seen on an urgent basis because they noticed hair falling out of their head during their shower that morning. They are panicked, as if it's the end of the world.

Now, let's examine how your Acquired Self uses experiences and information to create fear for itself. Your mind (your Acquired Self) is conditioned to create a mental picture of each and every experience. It doesn't matter if it's a real experience (your own experience) or a virtual experience (someone else's experience). It judges each experience as *happy* or *sad*, *good* or *bad*, *pleasurable* or *painful* according to the conditioning of the mind, based on *past experiences* and *information* acquired from stories, newspapers, books, magazines, TV or the internet. After judging, it stores the experience in the memory box where it stays alive, even years later.

Your Acquired Self <u>wants</u> more and more of those experiences which it judges to be *good*, *happy* or *pleasurable*. It does <u>not want</u> the ones it judges *sad*, *bad* or *unpleasant*.

Your Acquired Self gets very attached to pleasurable experiences associated with position, power, fame, success and victories. It wants more and more of these experiences. It does not want to lose them ever. *Even the idea of losing them creates fear.*

Your Acquired Self also wants to <u>avoid</u> unpleasant experiences such as those associated with failure, punishment, loneliness, humiliation, poverty and disease, etc. *Even the thought of unpleasant experiences triggers intense fear.*

It's interesting to note that your Acquired Self reacts to "hypothetical situations" that it creates itself. Pretty crazy, isn't it? In reality, those situations don't exist at all. It creates a threatening hypothetical situation and then tries to solve it. As the threat is hypothetical, so are all of the solutions. Your Acquired Self is so insecure and so afraid of its own death, that it creates all possible dreadful case scenarios and tries to figure out how it can escape its death in every possible way. In doing so, it keeps the virtual threat alive. How ironic! In this way, your Acquired Self creates tons of unnecessary fear for itself. When you totally identify with your Acquired Self, you experience all of this fear.

Isn't Fear Good for Us?

There is a myth that *"it's natural to have fear. It may even be good for us. It helps us to survive."* From the perspective of your Acquired Self, it is a perfect statement as we observed earlier in the book. Since a majority of people are in the grip of their Acquired Self, this kind of statement seems quite reasonable to them.

Let's take a close look at this concept using the logic that we are born with - the true intelligence in all human beings.

What happens when you are faced with a threat? Let's say you're walking through a forest and suddenly, you're face to face with a bear. You take immediate action *without thinking*. There is no time for thinking. Instantaneously, you either *fight* or *run away*. This intelligence resides in your body. It prepares you instantaneously by releasing a large amount of adrenaline in the blood stream, which raises your heart rate, blood pressure and blood glucose enabling you to deal with the situation immediately. You are physically primed to fight or run away. This is the so called *Fight or Flight* response, which happens instantaneously once you are faced with a real threat. With your immediate action, you will either survive or die. <u>So far there is no fear.</u>

Let's presume you survived the situation. A few moments later, you start thinking: *"What could have happened?!!" " I could have died or lost a leg and be paralyzed for the rest of my life. If I had died, what would have happened to my wife and kids?!."* Now intense fear sets in.

At the time of the actual threatening situation, there was no fear, but thinking about it creates fear.

It's the action at the time of the threatening situation that saves your life. So it is not fear, but your spontaneous action in a situation that may save your life.

Fear Actually Harms Your Body

The entire experience of facing the bear and your conditioned mind's *interpretation and reaction* gets stored in your memory box and becomes added to your Acquired Self.

Let's say a month later, you tell your story to a friend. It is basically your memory box repeating the stored event. Even though there is no bear in front of you, your conditioned mind sees a bear and warns your body of this virtual threat. Obviously, there is a big difference between the real bear and the virtual bear. *However, your body cannot distinguish between a real and virtual threat. It relies on your mind.* So if your mind sees a threat, so does your body. Therefore, your body responds to this virtual threat the same way as it did to the real threat: by releasing adrenaline. Your heart starts pounding, blood pressure rises and blood glucose rises. In addition, you also think "what might have happened" and this thinking creates a lot of fear. The net result: you have an unpleasant sensation of fear and physical symptoms of your heart pounding, a rise in blood pressure and blood sugar. Of course, your friends also join in with various thoughts of "what could have happened." They may tell you about a similar story they saw on TV or read in the newspaper. From these collective thoughts, you all build up a cloud of fear.

Now here is another interesting fact: **Since you can neither fight nor flee this virtual situation, the situation does not resolve.** Your body continues to release adrenaline as long as your memory (part of your Acquired Self) and your friends' stories continue to generate the virtual threat. You continue to experience fear and its damaging effects on the body as long as you have fearful thoughts. There is no resolution of the situation.

After tormenting you for a while, your Acquired Self (your memory and thoughts) settles back down in the memory box, ready to be awakened each time you talk or think about your deadly experience.

Fear Leads to High Blood Pressure, Diabetes, Heart Attacks and Autoimmune Diseases

Repeated episodes of fear not only release adrenaline,

227

but also another stress hormone, cortisol, from your adrenal glands. Frequent release of adrenaline and cortisol from your adrenal glands in response to fear can lead to a permanent rise in blood pressure and blood glucose. Then one day, your doctor tells you that you have hypertension or diabetes. If you already have heart disease, a flashback of a dreadful experience with a rush of adrenaline may actually cause an acute heart attack.

Fear also plays a major role in causing Autoimmune Diseases such as Asthma, Hashimoto's Thyroiditis, Graves' Disease, Type 1 Diabetes, Irritable Bowel Syndrome, Crohn's Disease, Ulcerative Colitis, Multiple Sclerosis, Lupus, Rheumatoid Arthritis, etc.

Let me explain how fear causes Autoimmune Diseases. Autoimmune means that your own immune system has gone crazy and is attacking your own organs as if they are alien and don't belong in your body. If your immune system attacks your lungs, you develop Asthma. If it attacks your pancreas, you develop Type 1 Diabetes… and so forth.

Why does the immune system go crazy? Normally, the immune system works to recognize real threats such as invading bacteria or viruses. It then mounts an attack to kill the invading organisms and then goes back to a *resting state*. However, if a person stays in the grip of an Acquired Self that is full of fear, then the immune system remains at *high alert* to fight off the virtual threat. However, there is no one to fight, so it starts to pick fights and destroys whatever organ it perceives as a threat. How ironic!

In order to attain security, it kills its own parts of the body.

Fear Causes Insomnia

Normally, the human mind and body function in harmony that sets up a biologic clock. At the crack of dawn, there is a surge in a number of hormones, such as cortisol, growth hormone and adrenaline, all of which act to increase your vigor, blood glucose and blood pressure. In other words, your mind prepares your body to go and do physical work, as our forefathers did for thousands and thousands of years.

As the day advances, these hormones (especially cortisol) go down. After sunset, cortisol is at very low level. With these hormonal changes, we feel tired and go to bed for a restful sleep. This is what endocrinologists call our *diurnal rhythm*. In layman's terms, it is our *biologic clock*.

Our modern lifestyle is obviously in conflict with our biologic clock. Most people don't wake up at the crack of dawn and don't go to bed hours after sunset. In the evening hours, most people watch TV or surf the internet. Most of this activity centers around fear, sensationalism and excitement, which results in a surge of adrenaline and cortisol. This obviously results in a *wound up* mind that does not want to shut up. The end result is insomnia.

Freedom From Insomnia

Often, people seek advice for their insomnia from a

physician who conveniently prescribes a sleeping pill, which forces sleep by causing chemical changes in the brain. However, these pills have a number of side-effects, including a potential for addiction. Neither you nor your physician looks at the root cause of insomnia. The efficacy of this band-aid approach is often short-lived. With the passage of time, these pills don't work as effectively as they did in the beginning. Then, you end up with higher doses and even multiple medications with a number of side-effects.

Once you have an insight about the whole mechanics of insomnia and see how your Acquired Self is at the root of your insomnia, you start to be free of your Acquired Self. Then, in the evening, you won't have the urge to watch TV or surf the internet. Instead, you might like to watch the sky, the stars and the clouds. You become aware of the "silence and stillness" of the night. Insomnia automatically vanishes away.

Fear Causes Chemical Changes in Your Brain

Since your early childhood, your Acquired Self continues to accumulate fearful stories from fiction books, history lessons and movies. It also tightly holds on to its own fearful experiences. Every day it adds more and more fearful experiences of itself and others. In this way, it creates an ever increasing "tower of fear" in your Acquired Self.

Your Acquired Self accumulates tons of fearful thoughts over the years and it loves to pile up more of them every day, which the Society Monster readily provides. That's why you love sensational stories from newspapers, TV, internet, other people, etc..

Over a period of time, the neuronal network of fear gets well established in your brain. Then reading, watching or listening to fearful news can trigger this well established network and result in a huge amount of fear, which causes chemical changes in your brain. In the milieu of these chemical changes, all of the old fearful experiences become alive, which feed in more fearful thoughts, which leads to more emotions of fear, more chemical changes and subsequently, more fearful thoughts. Thus, a vicious cycle sets in and you get consumed by fearful thoughts and emotions of fear, both reinforcing each other.

Fear Causes a Constant State of Unease and Nervousness

Your body responds to the constant bombardment of fearful thoughts and produces an excess release of adrenaline and cortisol. Consequently, many people get in a constant state of *unease, nervousness, hyperactivity*, *restlessness* and *agitation*. This is also commonly known as *nervous energy*, which can help you to accomplish a lot of tasks. Often, these people can't sit still more than a few minutes. They have to keep moving, keep doing, one thing after another. Sometimes, they are not even fully aware of their movements and actions. In general, they become good workers. Employers love them. However, at the end of the day, they are totally *exhausted*. Then, they look for different ways to boost up their energy, all of which have their own negative side-effects. They also often suffer from *headaches* and *insomnia*.

Many people get so used to their constant state of "unease and nervousness" that they think it's normal for them and there's nothing they can do about it.

Fear Causes Anxiety and Panic Attacks

Excess adrenaline causes symptoms of restlessness, agitation, insomnia, sweaty palms and palpitations. We label these symptoms as *Anxiety*.

If your root cause of anxiety remains untreated, as is often the case, you start to develop even more severe and dramatic symptoms such as chest tightness, air hunger, heart pounding, lump in the throat, excess perspiration, cold sweaty palms, and feeling of passing out. These symptoms, we label as *Panic Attacks.*

It is interesting to note the symptoms of Panic Attacks are identical to the symptoms of an actual heart attack and some other life-threatening medical conditions such as congestive heart failure or a clot in the lungs. Ironically, knowledge of these serious medical conditions actually frightens you even more and worsens your Panic Attacks. Obviously, many patients with Panic Attacks end up in the emergency room at a hospital.

Freedom from Nervousness, Anxiety and Panic Attacks

Typically after a physician diagnoses you with Anxiety Disorder or Panic Attack, you are prescribed an anti-anxiety drug which basically works by changing the chemicals in your brain and often gives you a temporary relief of symptoms. However, if the root cause of your anxiety is not treated, your anxiety continues like a smoldering fire ready to erupt into flame with any fearful news.

Most anti-anxiety drugs can cause a number of side-effects including an addiction to the drug. These drugs work as a band-aid. In time, if the root cause of your anxiety and panic attacks is not treated, you most likely will need higher doses of these medications and often will need to keep adding more and more of these drugs to cover up the *volcano* of your anxiety and panic attacks.

However, once you develop the insight that the *root cause of nervousness, anxiety and panic attacks actually resides inside you* as your Acquired Self, you realize that the *treatment also resides insides you.* The moment you can see your Acquired Self at the root of your anxiety, you start to be free of it.

Use logic and you realize that your own thoughts create a hypothetical situation which can be very frightening. With logic, you realize that it is all in your head. The situation is all hypothetical. It is a ghost, a phantom, an illusion, a monster in

233

your head; no more.

When you see the architect of fear clearly, do not run away, as it is only an illusion, not real at all. It can't harm you. While seeing your Monster in action, you also need to be fully aware of what is real: the present, the *Now* around you. *See* the objects around you and also be aware of the space in which they exist. *Listen* to sounds around you and be aware of the silence which gives rise to sounds. Pay attention to your breath by counting your inhalation and exhalation. You will see that slowly your Monster subsides and is replaced by a peaceful tranquility.

Phobias

Your Acquired Self often also thinks like this: *"I must never face this kind of dangerous situation again. What can I do to prevent it from happening again?"*

For example, if you had a bad experience in the wilderness, your Acquired Self may say, "*I should avoid going into the wild.*" It leads to "avoidance behavior." Sometimes, it may not even be your own experience. If you heard or read about the traumatic experience of others at airports or during flights, your Acquired Self may decide *Not* to take an airplane trip any more.

As a child, if you hear from your parents that someone died from a *bee sting*, you may become fearful of bees and avoid going to the park that you previously used to love to visit. Even worse, if you happened to be stung by a bee and your parents created a huge drama (even though nothing really happened to you), you will likely develop a phobia for insects.

Now don't take me wrong. Your parents take all of these measures out of their love for you, so *nothing bad should ever happen to you*. Just the thought of what could have happened to you because of a bee sting creates a lot of anxiety for your parents.

Often these traumatic, threatening experiences get pushed into the *subconscious* or even *unconscious* part of your psychological mind. On the surface, everything is fine, but you want to stay in total control. Certain situations where you don't have full control, such as in a crowd, an elevator or an airplane, can give rise to intense anxiety and even a panic attack. Then, you start to avoid crowds (which is called agoraphobia), or avoid closed spaces (which is called claustrophobia).

Fear Can Express as Anger and Hate

You had a bad experience and your conditioned mind doesn't want it to ever happen again. Therefore, it wants to stay in control all the time. Even the thought of losing control creates a huge amount of fear. Your Acquired Self wants security at all costs.

It may go an extra step to pursue security for itself and its loved ones. For instance, in the earlier example of encountering a bear, you may start to think, "Maybe I should also protect other humans from this nasty creature called a bear. I should look into joining a group that kills bears and similar beasts that endanger my fellow human beings."

In addition to fear, now you have also developed *hate* towards wild beasts. You may express this hate verbally, in writing or even physically. *This is how deep seated fear expresses itself as anger, rage and hate.*

Now imagine you meet a person or a group who due to their own Acquired Self, loves wild beasts and wants to protect them by spending taxpayer's (including yours) money. You start hating these kinds of people and groups. You may even join a group or a party that collectively hates wild beasts and wild-beast lovers. Now you have a mission in life. Each time you listen to a radio program in which so called experts talk about saving wild beasts, your blood starts boiling. You may even call the radio station and express your point of view. You may even be invited to one of these shows. You proudly tell your story and fight the other expert, who tells his story and opposes your point of view.

Your conditioned mind says "All these people who support my enemy, the wild animals, are also my enemy." Each time you have a flashback of your frightful experience as you talk or think about it, your body prepares to fight or flee by producing increased amounts of adrenaline.

In summary, fear is the underlying cause of psychological symptoms of uneasiness, jitteriness, restlessness, insomnia, anxiety, panic attacks, phobias, hate, anger and physical or verbal violence as well as physical symptoms of high blood pressure, high blood sugar, pounding of heart, chest tightness or pain, air hunger, feeling of passing out, and a long list of autoimmune diseases.

Fear Can be Addictive

An Adrenaline rush also gives you a feeling of excitement, but then this feeling goes away. Of course, you want more excitement. So you look for fear. Plenty of it is available in the form of sensational news in the media. You also get it by repeatedly talking to yourself or someone else about your bad experiences.

Your *monster of fear* also wants to infect others. In your social encounters, you love to talk about sensational, fearful stories. Other peoples' monsters readily jump in and validate your stories with their own stories. Soon you and your friends are sitting in a *cloud of fear* and loving it.

Next time, watch people talk at their workplace or at parties and notice how everyone joins in as soon as someone tells a fearful story. Everyone loves to outdo others by telling more intense fearful stories.

Sometimes, you decide to watch a scary movie to feed your appetite for fear. Most people become addicted to fear.

Fear Sells

In the grip of fear, you can't think with logic. You simply want security at any costs. The *Society Monster* knows it very well. So first it creates fear for you and then it can sell you whatever it wants, in the name of providing security. In this way, fear is actually very profitable and generates big business. These days the whole world revolves around it.

From your early childhood, the *Society Monster* downloads into your Acquired Self all sorts of fearful stories with the help of books and movies. In your adult life, the *Society Monster* continues to download tons of fearful stories with the help of news media, books, movies, internet, etc.

Once your Acquired Self has been fully primed with fear, it is eager to find security. Then your Society Monster starts to sell you *virtual security* in a never-ending list of "what you should do to be secure" and you gladly follow the instructions: *Gated communities, burglars alarms, health insurance, disability insurance and life insurance* are some examples.

Freedom from Fear

Only if people knew that fear is a product of their own conditioned mind. Then, they would realize that freedom from fear lies in freedom from their own conditioned mind, their Acquired Self.

Each time you are in the grip of fear, look at it instead of running away from it. It is virtual and really cannot harm you. However, you must be fully aware that it is your Acquired Self and not You, the True you. Only then you can look at it and see its true colors. Pay attention to your breathing. It helps to stay in the present moment, because breathing is a real act taking place in the Now. Soon, you will see your *fearful,* Acquired Self subsiding. That's why I sometimes call the Acquired Self a *parasite*: it needs to be fed from you. The moment it does not get its feed from you, it starts to die.

However, it may soon come back. After all, these are your life-long habits. It is quite persistent, clever and treacherous. However, in reality, it is virtual. That's why I also call it the *Monster.* Because it serves no purpose but to hurt you, I also call it the *enemy within.*

You need to stay alert, pay attention and clearly see each time this Monster wants to scare you. With time, this Monster will not have any control over you.

Here is an example to illustrate these points:

One of my friends asked for my advice, as she was having a lot of anxiety and insomnia. I asked her what kind of thoughts run through her mind. She said, "I worry a lot and I know that worrying is not good for my health, and you've told me that worrying can affect my immune system, but I can't help it. I have tried books, seen psychiatrists and am on anti-anxiety drugs, but

239

nothing is working any longer. I think I need another drug to calm my nerves."

I counseled her about the True Self and Acquired Self and that the freedom from the Acquired Self was the true cure for her anxiety disorder. "But how can I do it? I understand what you are saying, but I keep going back to anxiety," she said.

I gave her an example. "Suppose you have a five year old child and she gets tangled in a thorny bush and starts crying. You rescue her and tell her not to get tangled in that bush. Five minutes later, she is back in that thorny bush. You rescue her again and repeat your advice, don't you?" She replied, "Yes, of course." I told her, "Each time you find yourself tangled with a fearful thought, get out of it. And yes, five minutes later, you may find yourself lost in some fearful thought again and you simply free yourself again from it.

Your thought tells you that something bad may happen to you or your loved ones. However, ask yourself, "Is it really happening at this very moment?" Keep asking yourself. The answer will almost always be, "No, it's not happening right now."

Then ask yourself, "What's happening now?" Look around and see what's around you - what can you hear, smell, touch and taste. This is your field of awareness. Stay in it as much as you can and you will be free of fearful thoughts.

Once free of fearful thoughts, you will be free of anxiety and insomnia without using any medications. Once you are cured of anxiety, your immune system will also start to work normally again.

However, stay on your medications until you start living like this: Be aware of your thoughts, don't get tangled up with them and live in your field of awareness. It takes a while before you start to live like this. The more you put it into everyday living, the more you will stay in your field of awareness. However, if you just talk about it and don't put into your daily living, it won't work. In that case, it will simply be information and knowledge that becomes a part of your Acquired Self.

After a while, my friend was able to be free of anxiety and insomnia and did not need any anti-anxiety drug any longer.

Fear of Disease, Disability and Death

Fear of disease comes from fear of *losing health*. For example, you read in a magazine how someone developed cancer (lost his health) and died after a painful period of being in and out of the hospital. You store this virtual experience along with its sad emotions in your memory box. Next time you hear the word cancer on the evening news, it may trigger thoughts like "what if it happens to me" and the mind creates a long virtual movie of your potential painful experience. You may become so fearful that you end up losing sleep. Fear itself is detrimental to your health and plays a significant role in the development of a disease. What an irony!

Most people are fearful of dying. Others may say that they are not afraid of dying, but they don't want any pain or suffering due to a disease or disability. They would rather die peacefully in their sleep. They don't want to be in a wheelchair due to a stroke or be in chronic pain, say due to back injury.

Many people simply hate the idea of death and want to beat it at all costs. You read how someone is *battling* against such and such disease.

The Root Cause of Fear of Disease, Disability and Death

Have you ever wondered who it is in you who is afraid of disease, disability and death? It's your Acquired Self, isn't it? Your Acquired Self, being virtual in nature, is in constant fear of dying. It comes up with a variety of reasons why it shouldn't die. For example, it may say that it does not want to leave any loved ones behind, especially its children, although they may be grown ups and have their own children. It wants to live forever for one reason or another. It hates any change. It wants the *status quo* to continue. That's why it wants its health to continue. It wants to stay in control and does not want to be vulnerable. It especially does not want to be dependent on others. That's why it's afraid of disability.

However, in reality, everything keeps changing. So does health. One day you're healthy, the next day you're sick. One day

242

you're totally *independent.* The next day, you're disabled and totally *dependent* on others. Death is the ultimate reality we all face one day. However, to the Acquired Self, the idea of death is a threat to its own existence. That's why it *hates* death. Any reminder about the ultimate reality of death triggers a potential threat to its existence and this perceived threat produces fear. That's why your Acquired Self, disguised as you, fights disease (instead of working with the body to take care of it), hoping to avoid death forever.

In our society, death is perceived as something bad, terrible and therefore, highly undesirable. The *Collective Acquired Self of society* feeds your individual Acquired Self all the negativity around the word "DEATH." For example, the most severe form of penalty for a crime is the *death penalty.* You often read in the newspaper: the *wrongful death,* the *death toll,* the *premature death,* the *unexpected death, cheating death,* the *jaws of death.*

Your Acquired Self has been programmed to stay in control in order to be secure. However, it also keeps getting reminded that it can't stay in control forever. This sense of *inability to control* creates major fear which then can lead to symptoms of anxiety and panic attack.

Freedom from the Fear of Disease, Disability and Death

As most people are in the grip of their Acquired Self, they are in the grip of fear of disease, disability and death. If you use

243

logic, you realize that *birth and death* are tied together; two sides of one coin. *If you are born, you are going to die.* This is the *law of nature.* Once you clearly see this *law of birth and death*, you actually can be free of your conditioned mind, who wants to stay in denial of this very basic fact.

Once freed of the concept of living a disease free life forever, you actually start to experience life. Instead of wasting all your energy trying to defy disease and death and live in fear, you realize that at this very moment, you are alive. All you need to do is get rid of fear and start living every moment.

Chapter 30

Depression

Depression is a devastating condition. It robs you of a good quality of life. You don't feel like doing anything. You simply stay in a sad mood which leads to an overall negative attitude and behavior towards life. Your negative behavior often cuts you off from those who truly care for you. This makes you more depressed and works as a self-fulfilling prophecy. Sometimes, people become so depressed that they even resort to *suicide*.

Some people go through periods of low energy as a part of depression, followed by periods of high nervous energy due to underlying anxiety disorder. This is called *Bipolar Affective Disorder*.

Most people take medications to treat symptoms of depression. Often, they stay on these drugs forever or their symptoms relapse if they stop taking them. With the passage of time, patients usually need to change their drug or add more drugs to manage their depressive symptoms.

Anti-depression drugs usually have a number of potential side-effects. To deal with these side-effects, you end up on more drugs. Before you know it, you are on a long list of medicines, dealing with their side-effects and become a frequent visitor to

245

doctors' offices.

What is the Root Cause of Depression?

If you really want to be free of depression, you need to go deeper and look at the root cause of your depression, by using logic.

Why does a person feel depressed? Sometimes, it is due to an incident, event or situation, such as loss of a loved one. Sometimes, you get a chronic illness or you are in a bad situation at work or at home and there is no way out. Often, you don't even know why you are depressed.

When you say, "I am depressed," who is this "I" who is depressed? This "I" is your Acquired Self, isn't it? So who is actually depressed is your Acquired Self and as long as you completely identify with your Acquired Self, you will continue to be depressed.

Your Acquired Self contains a large pile of memories, *bad* memories as well as *sweet* memories, both of which can be at the root of your depression. Bad memories obviously create a lot of psychological pain for you. How about sweet memories? Well, sweet memories are the basis of "missing." For example, you love your daughter and have a lot of fond memories. Now she has grown up and moved away. Stuck in those sweet memories, you start to miss her. Sometimes "missing" can lead to depression.

Memories are the root cause of depression. Therefore, let's examine what a memory really is. *A memory is a snap shot of an event, with a story attached, an interpretation/judgment attached and a corresponding emotion attached.* In this way, memories are created by your own conditioned mind, your Acquired Self and therefore, it holds on to them as "My" memories and keeps them alive.

For example, you were humiliated in front of your class by your 2nd grade teacher. The event is long gone, but you still have a vivid picture of the entire event and can still feel the agonizing pain of humiliation. In reality, the event has died, but it is very much alive in your head with all of its fire of psychological pain.

Now consider this. Events are happening all the time. Your conditioned mind keeps making memories out of these events. Imagine the heavy burden of memories your conditioned mind has graciously generated for you. Within these memories lie your emotions of *worthlessness, sadness, loneliness, embarrassment* and *abandonment*.

Every emotion you have is basically a reaction to your thought. A bubbling volcano of these emotions creates chemical changes in your brain. This altered chemical environment is conducive to more negative thoughts. These negative thoughts then trigger more negative emotions and consequently, more negative thoughts, which results in an extremely vicious cycle of negative thoughts, negative emotions and associated chemical changes in the brain. This is what causes depression. It all starts from negative thoughts, which then lead to negative emotions and subsequent chemical changes in the brain.

Anti-depression drugs work by counteracting the chemical changes in your brain, but do not take care of the root cause: the thoughts which are kept alive as memories by your Acquired Self. *An analogy is going after the mosquitoes while the pond continues to widen.* That's why you end up adding more and more drugs as time goes by, in order to control your symptoms of depression.

It is worth noting that some painful events from your early childhood get so deep into your Acquired Self that you may not even recollect them, but they stay alive in your *unconscious mind*, a part of your Acquired Self. On the other hand, a lot of events you can easily recollect: we call it your *subconscious*, another part of your Acquired Self.

Hope as an Escape Mechanism

To escape from the relentless agony of memories, your mind can generate some positive thoughts it calls *hope*. In this way, it can temporarily stop the vicious cycle of negative thoughts, and negative emotions.

However, *hope* is often a temporary remedy. Sooner or later, your memories take over and you become depressed again. Many people go through swings of *hopefulness* and *hopelessness*.

"Stay Busy" as an Escape Mechanism

You may be advised to stay busy to ward off depression. Society has created proverbs such as "an empty mind is an evil mind." By staying busy, you actually try to run away from your memories. This escape mechanism also does not work for long. Sooner or later, you get stuck in your memories and become depressed again.

Other Escape Mechanisms: Excessive Eating, Excessive Work, Excessive Partying, Excessive Alcohol, Illegal Drugs, Smoking, Gambling

To find some relief from the agony of memories, your Acquired Self can run to some other escapes as well. These escapes can take the form of *excessive eating, excessive work, excessive partying, excessive alcohol, excessive sex, illegal drugs, smoking, pornography, gambling, etc.* Each escape has its own negative consequences. Obviously, these escapes do not free you of your painful memories.

True Freedom From Depression

Once you fully understand the root cause of your depression is your own Acquired Self, you stop running for escapes. Once you clearly see the architect of your depression is your own conditioned mind, your Acquired Self, you have a choice: stay in the grip of your Acquired Self and be depressed or

249

be free of your depression by dissociating from your Acquired Self.

Clearly see the virtual nature of your memories. Yes, events happened, but those events are not happening any more except in your head. In reality, *new* events happen all around you all the time, but you remain so trapped in your memories that you miss out most events in the *Now* such as the gentle breeze, the chirping birds and the twinkling stars.

Pay attention to the real events happening around you in your field of awareness which is: what you see, hear, smell, taste and touch. Then, you will be free from your memories. The more you stay in the *Now*, the more you will stay away from your memories.

Every now and then you may find yourself in the grip of your memories. However, then you will see the true nature of these memories: They are virtual, illusory, unreal. No more than bundles of thoughts and emotions. You will not believe in anything these memories imply. Why? Because none of them are happening right now. Hence, there is no need to run away, change or make sense out of those events from the so called "past." Just see them for what they are: ghosts swirling in your head. That's all! That's how your depression automatically ends.

Caution: *Please do not stop any medicine without consulting your doctor.*

250

Chapter 31

Grief

Grief is a deep sense of loss, usually loss of someone or something very *close* to you. It could be the death of a loved one. It could be loss of your health or looks. It could be the loss of a possession such as your precious jewelry, car or house. It could be loss of your job, savings or pension plan. It could be loss of your friendship, marriage, partnership or it could be loss of your political or religious philosophy.

Grief is quite painful. Many people can't stand it and end up with depression. Some may try to suppress these emotions through denial and eventually end up with *emptiness, restlessness* and *anxiety*. Some try various escape mechanisms which are only temporary fixes and often cause more trouble.

What is the Root Cause of Grief?

In order to be free of grief, you need to go deeper and find the root cause of grief. Use logic and you realize that grief comes from the loss of someone or something that you were very attached to. Someone or something that had become an integral part of "you." In fact, what you think is "you" in not you, but your Acquired Self. Actually it is your Acquired Self who is *bruised,* because part of it is gone or taken away.

251

True Freedom from Grief

While feeling grief, can you also be aware that it is your Acquired Self who is grieving? The moment you disassociate yourself from your Acquired Self, you will feel relief from grief. *But do not deny or suppress grief.* It will only make matters worse. Fully feel the pains of grief, but also be alert and realize that it is your Acquired Self who is hurt and grieving.

Pay attention to the *Now*, your field of awareness. Experience every moment of life inside you and around you. Then, you realize you are actually part of the *Now*. You feel an amazing inner peace. This is your True Self!

Chapter 32

Lack of Trust, Paranoia and Psychosis

What is trust? What do you really mean when you say "I trust you." Don't you imply that I expect you to behave in certain ways and *not* to behave in certain other ways? In this way, trust actually implies expectations at a deep level. For example, if I tell my child, "I trust you to finish your homework," what I really mean is that I expect her to finish her homework or I will be disappointed. When you trust someone, you basically expect a certain kind of behavior from that person.

Your expectations are very *deep* when you trust someone, and therefore, if your expectations are not met, you get hurt *deeply*. For example, if your trusted friend betrays you, it is more hurtful than if some colleague doesn't live up to your expectations. Trust is one of the foundations of marriage. You expect your spouse to be faithful. However, if your spouse does cheat, you are badly hurt.

What is the Root Cause of Lack of Trust, Paranoia and Psychosis?

Let's take a close look at the origin of deep expectations and trust. These deep expectations start in our early childhood. Babies start to trust their parents, because they are always there

253

to fulfill their needs, physical as well as psychological. Now, what happens if one day you decide to leave your little one to the care of a babysitter? Your baby cries and cries. What happens? The trust is *broken,* as your baby feels *abandoned.* You know you are only leaving for a short time, but for the baby, you may never come back. Your child's deep expectation of you being there forever is *broken.* Therefore, she cries and cries. After a few hours, you are back. Now you are again there to fulfill all of her physical as well as psychological needs until the next episode of "babysitting.'" During this time, your baby's trust in you is restored, although not completely, because the previous traumatic experience of *abandoning* is simply pushed down into the unconscious.

You may also have to go out of town as a part of your job. Some parents have to leave their children for an extended period of time, months or even years, in order to earn a living for the family. Parents think they are making a sacrifice for the family, but their children do not understand this sacrifice. All they know is that their loving dad (or mom) is not around to play with them or take care of them. They trusted you to always be there, but you broke their trust.

As your child grows up, sooner or later you find the urge to discipline your child for bad behavior. You may use harsh words or physically strike your child. In addition to physical trauma, your child's Acquired Self is deeply hurt, as he trusted you to be a *loving* person. "How could you hurt me while I trusted you to love and take care of me?" an inner voice silently

254

questions. The more your child is attached to you, the more she is going to get hurt each time you break her trust by abandoning her or by punishing her.

As an adult, the Acquired Self often gets attached to a certain political, cultural or religious philosophy. This creates trust and strong expectations, which sooner or later, are not met and leads to a huge amount of mistrust and anger. That's how some people get angry at *God*.

The repeated episodes of *trust shattering experiences* continue to pile up into the Acquired Self at the unconscious and subconscious level and remain very much *alive* there, although a person may or may not remember them. The *Unconscious* consists of emotional experiences from very early childhood which cannot be remembered. The *Subconscious* consists of emotional experiences from later childhood and adult life, which ordinarily remain under the surface of consciousness, but can be easily recalled.

The Acquired Self keeps these unconscious as well as subconscious traumatic experiences alive and seriously taints a person's perspective. A person with a heavy load of this kind of emotional experience may never be able to engage in a truly trusting relationship with a spouse, child, neighbor or coworker.

Paranoia

Lack of trust can take a more severe form to the point

255

that a person not only mistrusts someone, but also becomes suspicious of them. This we call *paranoia*.

Where does this layer of suspicion come from? If you look at it closely, you find that it often starts in early childhood as well. Overly protective parents download *suspicion* into the growing Acquired Self of their children. "Never trust any stranger. They may harm you." This phrase is often told to children growing up in the western hemisphere. The idea of suspicion continues to be drilled in the growing Acquired Self of a lot of individuals. For some, these ideas of suspicion can take an extreme form and they become *paranoid*.

Psychosis

In the grip of the Acquired Self, such a person obviously looks at others with suspicion. Such a person may start to believe that others are out there to harm him. This leads to *delusional thinking*, which may then affect the behavior of these individuals as well.

These people start to protect themselves from mind-made dangers and threats. For example, a person may decide to leave her home, because she believes others in the house may harm her. A person may decide to never shake hands with others in order to protect against those nasty germs that may kill her. This kind of severely abnormal, delusional thinking and totally irrational behavior is what we label as '"Psychosis." In simple language, it is called madness or insanity. Such a person is "out of touch with reality."

Often such a person avoids social interactions, as the mind is overwhelmed with suspicious thoughts. From these thoughts arise more convoluted and delusional thoughts based upon what else is in the content of the Acquired Self. For example, a person may declare they are *talking to God* or acting under the *directions of God*. Sometimes, the thoughts can be so overwhelming that a person may start seeing or hearing imaginary things or events. This we label as *"hallucinations."* Actions arising out of delusion and hallucinations can harm oneself or others. The whole streak of paranoia and delusional thinking is supposed to protect you, but you may actually seriously hurt yourself and those who truly care for you. How ironic!

Delusions and hallucinations are created by the Acquired Self and such a person completely identifies with her Acquired Self. Therefore, to that person, these delusions and hallucinations are real, although everyone else can see them as unreal and imaginary.

True Freedom From Mistrust, Paranoia and Psychosis

Is it possible to be free of mistrust, paranoia and psychosis? Most people think it is not possible. Doctors treat psychosis with medications, usually on a long term basis. Despite medications, many people continue to have delusions and irrational behavior. Then doctors add more medications. Some are locked up in mental hospitals for life. Each drug has its own potential serious side-effects.

Note: Please do not stop taking your medications without the advice of your doctor.

If you seriously want to be rid of mistrust, paranoia and psychosis, you have to look deeply. What is at the root of these psychological disorders? If you dig deeply, you will find that the culprit is the Acquired Self - the conditioned mind, the emotional experiences and the thoughts swirling in the head. When a person is in the tight grip of his Acquired Self and completely identifies with it, he gets totally lost in his thoughts and emotions. He loses touch with reality and lives in a *virtual land* of his own. This is the basis of insanity. This is the basis of psychosis.

In order to be free of paranoia and psychosis, you have to be free of your Acquired Self. Only then you will realize that all of the mistrust, anger and suspicion is only in your conditioned head, keeping you away from reality. Simply use logic and you can be free of your Acquired Self. Then there are no expectations, no trust or mistrust, no suspicion, no enemies, no one to be afraid of. In this way, you can be completely free of mistrust, paranoia and psychosis.

Chapter 33

Attention Deficit Disorder (ADD)

A number of people get the diagnosis of Attention Deficit Disorder (ADD) and receive prescription drugs to treat it. Symptoms can be controlled as long as you take medications, but recur if you stop the drugs. In this way, treatment is superficial and temporary. Is it possible to be free of ADD without taking any drugs? Before you can answer this question, you need to look deeper at the <u>root cause</u> of ADD.

What is the Root Cause of Attention Deficit Disorder (ADD) ?

The name, Attention Deficit Disorder basically describes the root cause of this disorder: attention deficit, lack of attention. Why doesn't someone pay attention? Because he has a busy mind. Now, what is a busy mind? It's your Acquired Self, isn't it? Hence, the root cause of ADD is your own Acquired Self.

Let's see how a person develops a busy mind. As we observed earlier in the book, the busy mind is a product of the conditioning of your mind by society, which starts in early childhood (and never stops), in the form of video games, talking toys, books, movies, etc. Your parents are instructed by the Collective Acquired Self of their society to provide you with as much mental stimulation as possible, in order for you not to be left

259

behind. This *mental stimulation* gets into high gear as you enter school and continues throughout your life. Overloaded with all kinds of stories, ideas, concepts and information, your mind gets all scattered. It runs in different directions like a wild horse. Your behavior, arising out of incessant, uncontrollable thoughts, becomes impulsive, reckless and at times, destructive. You are easily distracted. Often, you stay in your own virtual world created by the busy mind. This often leads to learning difficulties in school.

Behavioral problems and learning difficulties get the attention of your teachers and your parents. Typically, your parents take you to your pediatrician, who diagnoses you with ADD and prescribes a medicine to control the symptoms. In this way, the root cause, your Acquired Self, conveniently escapes detection and you continue to suffer from ADD throughout your life.

True Freedom from Attention Deficit Disorder (ADD)

Once you realize your Acquired Self is the root cause of your ADD, you can treat it by freeing yourself from your Acquired Self. Realize that the Acquired Self is not truly who you are.

Guided Practice

Here is a *guide* you can follow:

- Sit quietly in a comfortable chair and relax. No music,

telephone, TV or any other distractions.

- Pay attention to your surroundings: what you see, hear, smell, taste and touch.

- Pay attention to *space* in which everything is, *silence* which gives rise to all sounds, and *stillness* in which all events take place.

- Pay attention to your breathing. Observe how your chest expands with inhalation and retracts with exhalation. Count your breaths.

- Pay attention to your mind. See how thoughts are chasing each other. Treat them as thoughts and no more. They are thoughts, but not *you*. Whatever they imply is not happening right now, in front of your eyes. Hence, it is virtual, unreal.

- Choose to stay out of the virtual world created by thoughts. Instead, choose to stay in the real world all around you, created by your five senses.

- Feel the *relief, inner peace* and *joy* once you are not in the grip of your thoughts.

- After a few moments of being in the *present,* you will likely be consumed by the thoughts again. It is okay.

261

Simply realize how your attention was hijacked by the thoughts. Bring your attention back to the *Present*, the *Now,* all around you.

- You will see how your attention shifts between the <u>unreal</u> world in your head and the <u>real</u> world all around you.

- Continue the practice. Don't get discouraged.

<u>Caution:</u>

Please do not stop your medications without consulting your physician.

Chapter 34

Stress Due to the Collective Acquired Self

People living in different cultures have different psychological patterns. The more insulated a culture is from other cultures, the more it has its own unique psychological characteristics.

Stress Arising Out of the Collective Acquired Self

The Collective Acquired Self instills the concept of collective *Pride*. It programs your Acquired Self to consider itself special because you belong to a certain culture, religion, nationality, etc. In this way, it cunningly creates a psychological wall of separation along the lines of culture, religion, society, or nationality. Obviously, this gives rise to collective *egotism*, *prejudice*, and *bias*. When you totally identify with your Acquired Self, you believe in this psychological division and suffer from *egotism*, *prejudice* and *bias*.

In addition, the Collective Acquired Self also feels the need to protect itself from others. This obviously leads to the concept of "Us against Them," which leads to collective *fear*, *hate* and *grievances* and often become the basis of battles and wars.

263

In the grip of your Acquired Self, you as an individual, suffer from these negative emotions as well.

Freedom from Collective Negative Emotions

Once you fully realize the root cause of Collective egotism, bias, prejudice, fear, hate and grievances is the Collective Acquired Self, you become free of it. This realization has a tremendous healing effect on you. Not only are you relieved of tons of your own stress, you don't create any more stress for others. Once you understand there are no "Us" and there are no "Others," you can see the truth that everyone is a human being. Then, you realize no one is special. There are no friends and no enemies. This is how egotism, prejudice, hate and fear ends automatically.

It is interesting to note the Collective Acquired Self gives you concepts of collective egotism, prejudice, hate and fear. At the same time, it also gives you concepts of humility, tolerance, peace and love. Obviously, these seemingly noble concepts do not work. That is why humans continue to be hateful, revengeful, fearful, greedy, selfish and jealous, despite theses noble concepts. Why? Because these concepts become part of the Acquired Self.

Equipped with these *two sets of contradictory concepts*, your individual as well as collective Acquired Self uses them according to its own psychological needs. This is the basis of double standards, rationalization, justifications, etc.

Chapter 35

Genetics

In medicine, we recognize that genetics plays an important role in causing many psychological and physical disorders. Geneticists also tell us there are increased chances that a certain genetic disorder will express itself in an individual, whose parents are blood relatives.

What Genetics Really Is

Let's use logic and look at genetics. Let's say a boy's mother was overprotective raising him and that led to him being *paranoid*. Why was she overprotective? Doesn't it shed some light on her own Acquired Self being suspicious and paranoid? It may be that her own mother was also a paranoid person and she learned all of her paranoid behavior from her mother.

A physician may look at it as an inherited trait without fully realizing that it is simply a *perpetuation of a learned behavior, an Acquired Self propagating from one generation to another.*

In addition, the body functions as one unit. Through the Mind-Body connection, your thoughts and emotions affect your entire body, including your eggs and sperms. In this way, you not only transfer your physical characteristics, but your psychological

Acquired Self as well.

Your Acquired Self also affects your physical health. A stressed out mind leads to a stressed out body. In this way, the Acquired Self plays a significant role in causing many physical illnesses, especially autoimmune diseases such as Type 1 diabetes, Hashimoto's thyroiditis, asthma, ulcerative colitis, Crohn's disease, rheumatoid arthritis, etc.; Fear creates a virtual threat and thereby keeps the immune system at "high alert" level, even though there are no real threats. Then, activated "soldiers" of the immune system have to kill someone. If they kill thyroid cells, you develop Hashimoto's thyroiditis, if they kill insulin producing cells, you develop Type 1 diabetes and so forth.

Because the body functions as one unit, sperms and eggs get the imprints of all of this drama of virtual threat and transfer these disorders into the next generation.

Thus, the propagation of the Acquired Self underlies the genetic predisposition to medical as well as psychological disorders.

Certain medical conditions are more prevalent in certain ethnic groups - groups that typically encourage marriages within its group members. These ethnic groups are very much attached to their collective identity, the Collective Acquired Self, with all of it's collective emotional burden. In this way, all of the ill effects of emotional stress on sperms and eggs are passed on to the next generation. After a few generations, these detrimental effects on sperms and eggs become well established and are the basis of genetic predisposition to certain psychological and physical diseases.

Genetic Acquired Self

In fact, you are born with a genetically determined *psychological self*, which carries all of the stress transmitted through generations. In this way, you carry all the imprints, including all of the emotional stress, from day one of the *beginning of life*. During your lifetime, you acquire more concepts, ideas, experiences and emotions as your own Acquired Self. Then, you conveniently pass onto your children all of the emotional burden since the beginning of time plus the emotional baggage you accumulate during your lifetime.

Can We Change Our Genetics?

We can be free of our Acquired Self and all it's associated emotional burden. Then our body, working as one unit, starts to heal. All the cells in the body, including sperms and eggs, start to rejuvenate, getting rid of the ill effects caused by the psychodrama of the Acquired Self through the generations. Then obviously, our eggs and sperms do not carry the ill effects onto the next generation. That's how we can change our genetics for the next generation.

Step 2

Freedom from the Conceptual World

Chapter 36

We Live in a Conceptual, Virtual World

Have you ever pondered at the world we live in? If you take a fresh, logical look at the human world without preconceived notions, you'll find that we live in a *conceptual world*, a *virtual world*, not a real world.

Because everyone around us lives in this conceptual, virtual world, we think it is real. Actually, we simply accept it as real and don't even bother investigating whether it is real or not.

For example, you're watching some movie awards on television. Through the goggles of the conditioned mind, ie. your Acquired Self, you see five actresses nominated for best actress. After a few moments of agony, they finally announce the *best actress of the year*. She obviously is thrilled and excited. Meanwhile, the other four feel defeated, though they try to force a fake smile. For the winner, the moment has finally arrived, the moment for which she waited for years. She gets overwhelmed with emotions, but manages to deliver an emotional speech and then her moment is over. In a few minutes, there is another winner (and losers) going through similar emotions.

269

If you're a serious moviegoer, you have your own opinion as to *who deserves the best actress award.* If the winner is the same as your choice, you're also *thrilled,* but if your choice loses, you're *disappointed,* sometimes even *angry* and *bitter* about the *unfairness of it all!* You sit through three hours of the show to get several moments of *excitement* and *disappointment.*

You and the world call it *entertainment.* You want more of it and the world is well equipped to provide you with more! Over the next several days, you enjoy reading more about the whole event on the internet, newspapers and magazines. There are stories behind the scenes, walking the red carpet, before and after parties, who wore what, who said what and on and on.

For the next few days, you even talk to your friends about the whole experience and have more fun. Actually, the more you know, the more you can impress your friends and the more special you feel about yourself.

Now, let's look at the whole event from an *unconditioned mind.* What you observe is a human being coming on stage to receive a shiny peace of metal. Holding that peace of metal in her hands, she gets very emotional, her eyes tearful, her voice choking. Why, you wonder? She says a few words and then everyone starts clapping. Why?

Obviously, that piece of metal has a huge *concept* attached to it. The human being appearing on stage is not just a

270

human being, but has a huge *concept* attached to her. The whole event has a huge *concept* attached to it. *The entire concept reverberates with the concept in your head (and in everyone else's head), about awards, actresses, actors, movies and the concepts of success, achievement, fame, wealth and glamour.*

In other words, your Acquired Self, the baby Monster, gets fed by the papa monster of society! That's why you enjoy it so much. For you and everyone else, it becomes real. Actually, you don't even question whether it is real or not. You watch and talk about it as if it was real.

It is interesting to know that you may be able to see the superficial, virtual nature of the part of the conceptual world that you are not attached to. For example, if you are attached to sports, but not to movies, you may not be interested in watching movie award shows. You may even recognize their superficial nature, but you won't miss the Super bowl, the US open, the World cup, the Olympics, etc. Each one of these has a huge concept attached to it - the concepts of *victory, achievement, fame, wealth and glamour.*

If you use logic, you realize that most sports are about a ball that is kicked, thrown, carried or hit. But the world doesn't see it that way. It sees these sports as a matter of *competition, victory, achievement, fame, wealth and glamour.*

By now, you may understand the virtual, conceptual nature of these events. However, you think these are occasional

271

events in your life. Well, take a closer look at the usual activities of your daily life. Most people spend most of their life in the realm of the conceptual, virtual world.

Here are some examples:
(*Let me first clearly state that I am making these observations using simple logic. I am not criticizing, putting down or making fun of any of these concepts.*)

The Internet, TV, newspapers and magazines obviously take you into the virtual, conceptual world: Many people start their day reading the newspaper or watching the morning news. Then they glance through magazines and surf the internet during the rest of the day. In the evening, they usually watch TV, play video games or surf the internet.

It's interesting to see some older people complaining about young people wasting too much time surfing the internet, playing video games or texting on their cell phone. Meanwhile, these "oldsters" spend their time reading newspapers or books, watching TV and talking about politics or religion.

Everything you read in newspapers, magazines or books as well as what you watch on TV or the Internet is conceptual and virtual, isn't it?

Everything you see in movies, stage shows, museums and art galleries is conceptual, isn't it? All pictures, paintings and statues are obviously conceptual.

All knowledge, whether history, mathematics, science, medicine, arts, geography or business is virtual and conceptual, isn't it?! In this way, all of our educational system is conceptual.

Language itself is conceptual. Observe how every word carries a concept with it. A few examples: Love, hate, romance, good, bad, beautiful, ugly, peace, war, cancer, death. In reality, spoken words are no more than sounds, but of course, each word has a concept attached to it. You can easily appreciate it when you listen to some language that you have not *learned*. Obviously, what you hear is sounds and that's all. You do not understand the meaning, the concepts attached to these sounds.

How about political systems? All are conceptual, aren't they?

How about religious establishments? They are all conceptual, aren't they?

How about cultures, traditions and values? They are all conceptual as well.

In reality, you see mountains, land, buildings, roads, trees, sky, clouds and water. However, on a map, you see continents, countries, states, provinces and cities - all conceptual.

How about marriage, romance, engagement, divorce? All are concepts, aren't they?

273

How about time? Seconds, minutes, hours, days, weeks, months and years. All conceptual. Different cultures have created different calendars.

How about national, religious and cultural holidays? All conceptual.

How about money? This concept is so overwhelming that no one ever thinks of it as conceptual.

Concept of Money and Economy

Almost everyone is in the grip of the concept of money and the economy. What is economy? It's a concept isn't it? You can't see the economy. You see currency, which itself is a concept. One dollar, 10 dollars, one sterling, 100 pounds, one Rupee, 1000 pesos, etc.

Give a 100 dollar bill to a one year old child. That child will probably chew it up or rip it apart. Why? Because infants have no concept of money. However, give the same 100 dollar to a teenager. That teen will be thrilled to have it. Why? Because teenagers have acquired the concept of money. In reality, it's only a piece of paper, but there is a powerful concept attached to it.

There are also concepts attached to gold, platinum, emeralds, diamonds, etc. In fact, these are simply metals and rocks, but there are huge concepts attached to them.

274

Every one wants to make money. Money itself is a concept. However, people don't think of it that way. To them, money is very real. *"You can't do anything without money,"* you argue. That argument still does not make it real. Money *may be necessary, to some extent, but it is not real. To live in the conceptual world, you need money, but it still does not make it real.*

If you look deeper, money is a way for humans to trade with each other. Not too long ago, people also used chickens, eggs, rice, etc., to purchase services from others. Animals don't trade.

Obviously, humans developed the *concept of trading.* The concept of trading came into being when humans started living in communities: the dawn of civilization. Humans got into the concept of "I, My, Me, Mine." For example, "I can exchange My eggs for Your wheat." Initially, it served a purpose, but then it took over the human race.

The concept of precious metals and money came into being. The more money (or precious metals) you had, the more you could buy. Initially, you bought things of necessity: food, clothes, houses. But this was not enough. You wanted to acquire more and more. Why? Because society also created other concepts - concepts of prestige, fame, glamour, enjoyment, entertainment, vacations and power. The more money you have, the more powerful, the more famous and the more prestigious you are.

With money, you can purchase various conceptual objects: your dream car, your dream home, your dream vacation, etc. Money is no longer a means to buy things of basic necessities. It is often used to enhance your ego.

"Wanting more" is the driving force behind the concept of money, but there is never enough of it when you're in the grip of "wanting more." Even a billionaire wants more money!

What's Wrong with the Concepts?

There is nothing inherently wrong with concepts. It is only when they are not treated as concepts, but as reality, that they become problematic and create stress for you and others.

Use logic and you realize that *concepts are not reality and reality is not conceptual*. However, most of humanity is lost in concepts and believes in them as if they were absolute truth. They get attached to them. They either love them (positive attachment) or hate them (negative attachment). Then, actions arise out of these attachments. Actions arising out of concepts create huge amounts of stress for you as well as everyone else.

Concepts also divide human beings into groups. Each group believes their own concepts to be true. This obviously creates *conflict*. One group sees the other group as a *threat* to their collective belief system, which often leads to violence: verbal

276

as well as physical and can even lead to battles and wars.

The Origin of Concepts

Concepts have created the conceptual world. A conceptual world exists out there as a Collective Acquired Self of society and inside each person as an individual Acquired Self. This is the basis of "stress" inside an individual as well as in the society at large and ultimately the whole world.

If concepts are at the root of stress, don't we need to dig deeper and find the origin of concepts?

Use logic and you realize all concepts are a product of the human mind. Animals don't have concepts. Why do humans have concepts?

Obviously, individuals acquire concepts from their collective concepts of their society. Then, individuals make sure they instill these concepts into their children. That's how these collective concepts are perpetuated. Some individuals also keep adding more concepts into the collective belief systems of the society. These individuals are usually called philosophers, intellectuals, teachers, gurus and leaders.

In order to get to the roots of concepts, you obviously need to look at the *origin of concepts.* How and when did concepts get started? Was there a time period when there were no concepts? What was the psychological state of humans when

277

there were no concepts?

Evolution of the Human Mind

Pondering these questions, one day I suddenly found the answers. Let me share my discovery with you. *Obviously, you may or may not agree!*

I realized that every human replicates the entire *journey of evolution.* Every human goes through the *stages of development* that humans collectively went through over a period of billions of years.

Scientists tell us life started in water (in the ocean) from one cell. Some organisms still continue to be one-celled organisms, such as amoebae, viruses and bacteria. Some of the one cell organisms developed into organisms comprised of two, four, and more and more cells.

Now let's look at how each and every human replicates this phenomenon. Each human starts life from one cell, in the *waters of the womb.* One cell divides into two, which divide into four and this proliferation of cells continues. During the nine months of development in the womb, one can see an embryo going through so many stages - sometimes it looks like a tadpole, sometimes like a fish, etc. What I see is an embryo replicating all the early stages of development that humans collectively went through. Only the period of millions of years is condensed into nine months.

Scientists also tell us that for some unknown reasons, certain life forms from the ocean were forced to live on land. Initially, they didn't like it. Many of them perished. However, slowly they adapted to live on the land. Slowly, they also developed the ability to crawl, sit, stand and walk. *So does a baby*: She leaves the womb at birth. Initially, she doesn't like it and cries a lot. However, as soon as she finds warmth and food, she is fine. Slowly, she starts to sit, crawl, stand and eventually walk. If you observe a baby going through these stages, you see that she puts out a huge effort to advance from one stage to the next. She is relentless, does not give up. *So did early humans*. They put out great effort to advance from one stage to another.

Millions of years of collective human great efforts are compressed into a couple of years of a baby's life. *If you observe, in the first couple of years of a baby's life, there is no language and there are no concepts. And there is no psychological stress. Once basic needs are met i.e. a full stomach, a clean diaper and a warm blanket, the baby is joyful and content. Wanting more (greed) does not exist. She is not thinking about the future - that's why she has no fear. She has no past - that's why she has no sadness, guilt, anger, grief or bitterness. She does not see any nationalities, religion, races or customs. That's why there is no bias, prejudice, hate or grievances.*

We can clearly see the stages of collective human development through the stages of development in a baby. *In this way, we can see there was a period in human development when*

*there were no languages and there were no concepts. Humans
lived in harmony. There were no divisions. They were joyful and
content. They had no past, no future.* They had no hate, no anger,
no bitterness, no jealousy. No one was fearful.

During the first couple of years, a baby doesn't speak, but
she is not dumb. Actually, she is very *intelligent* right from birth.
Place a hour old baby on her mother's chest and she will find a
nipple in no time and start suckling. *She knows exactly where to
find her food.* She obviously does not go to school to learn this.
She is born with this intelligence. She is curious - looking and
observing everything.

During the corresponding stage in collective human
development, humans were intelligent and curious. Through their
curiosity, they slowly started to develop simple tools. This was
the *beginning of technology.* They simply used intelligence and
curiosity to develop simple real tools.

With these tools, they were able to hunt food more easily.
This *reward* encouraged more technology. They had to use their
brain more in order to develop more technology. *This led to the
evolution of the brain.* The evolving brain was able to produce
more technology and this led to the cycle of positive feedback:
more technology caused more brain development, which led to
more technology. You can see this in toddlers. Those who are
given more mental challenges go through brain development
faster compared to those who receive little mental challenges.

During mental development of a child, language comes at a much later stage. Their first words are simple and basically help to communicate very basic needs: "water, pee-pee, poo-poo." Gradually, the child acquires more and more vocabulary. Every word has a concept attached to it. That's how she acquires concepts. With age, she learns more complex words and the complex concepts attached to these words.

Thus, we can see that in collective human development, language started at a much later stage. Initially, it was very simple – mono-syllables, mostly communicating needs. Gradually, it became more complex, ultimately giving rise to highly complex concepts.

One of the earliest concepts a child develops is "I, Me, My, Mine." In collective human development, this was probably the earliest concept. *It's a concept that would change humans forever.* Gradually, humans kept adding more concepts as they started living in communities.

With the birth of civilization, more concepts developed as a necessity for society to function. Initially, these concepts were simple, but then these concepts overtook the human mind and enslaved it. The *"genie of concepts"* has continued to grow over time and is in high gear at the present time.

The concept of "I, Me, My, Mine" is at the core of all other concepts. These concepts have created a lot of stress for humans as well as other life forms on the planet.

281

However, as you can see, it really is no one's fault. It's simply a <u>by-product</u> of the evolution of the human mind.

It's interesting to note that from time to time, some individuals can see the collective sufferings humans have brought on each other and they can also see that concepts are at the root of these sufferings. Ironically, they come up with their own concept in the form of a philosophy, theory, dogma, etc. which simply adds to the pile of concepts and ultimately, creates more sufferings.

In the last five thousand years or so of known human history, man's psychology has not changed. He continues to be greedy, angry, hateful, jealous and fearful despite the birth of a number of religious, social and political philosophies. Why? Because all of these philosophies became part of the collective pile of concepts.

The Multilayered Tower of the Conceptual World.

The conceptual world, in your head, as well as in society, has many layers. It continues to add more and more layers. You can clearly see how *tiers* of concepts are added to the growing tower of the conceptual world in an individual, as a person grows from a child into a teenager, an adult and then an elderly person. And also in a society when it advances from a primitive to a modern society.

At the bottom layer are some early, simple concepts that you see in young children such as "my parents, my siblings, my food items, my clothes." You also see these simple concepts in so called primitive societies. In other words, the earlier layers of concept are simple and consist of concepts which are attached to *real* objects.

With time, other layers of concepts are added into the heads of individuals as well as into the collective heads of societies going through modernization. *Many of these concepts are attached to other concepts.* Often, there are several layers of conceptuality.

For example, when you watch a movie, the picture on the screen is not real, but an illusion, a concept. Obviously, there are no *real* people walking or talking on the screen. The story, with its characters, creates another layer of concept.

For example, in real life there is a real person, labeled with the concept of *prince*. In the movie, the writer creates a *virtual prince*: a concept attached to a concept. Animation is another layer of concept. Creating hypothetical creatures, objects and planets is another layer of concept. Then, you read the movie's reviews in the newspapers, which adds another layer of concept. The movie's success in terms of money is another concept. If the movie wins an award, that's another layer of concept.

With the progress of technology, we are adding more and

283

more layers of concepts. Just in the last 100 years or so, we have seen an explosion of the conceptual world, starting with electricity, automobiles and airplanes, progressing into motion pictures, radio and TV and advancing into computers, the internet and cell phones. As you can see, concepts are becoming more and more multilayered and complex.

It's No One's Fault

It is important to realize that the conceptual world is simply a byproduct of the evolution of the human mind. Therefore, it is no one's fault.

Chapter 37

The Human Mind

The evolved human mind has three components:

1. The Technological Mind

As a product of our evolution, we humans developed a technological mind which was useful for our survival. For example, we built tools and grew plants. The results were rewarding, so this technological mind continued to evolve and is still continuing to evolve. While this mind is responsible for our tremendous technological progress, it also gave us a huge psychological burden. Call it a side-effect of the evolution of the human mind.

2. Conceptual, Conditioned, Thinking Mind

Slowly, the human mind developed another component, the thinking mind. This started *concepts*. Perhaps the first concept was, "I, Me, My and Mine" which also readily changed into "We, Us and Ours."

Due to tools, man was able to survive longer. He didn't have to find caves or hunt and gather food all the time. He was able to build homes, grow plants and live collectively to fend off dangers such as other animals. This led to the *dawn of civilization*, which then gave rise to *language*, certain *rules* and distribution of *tasks*. This is how societies evolved.

Some clever men with more evolved thinking minds also saw an opportunity to take advantage of the others and hierarchy came into existence. Caste systems developed. Each society got divided into certain layers: peasants, soldiers, elite, the ruling class and the head of the tribe. Political and religious organizations came into being to control the masses.

These concepts gradually separated humans from nature and then gradually divided humans into tribes. The evolving mind wanted more food, more land, more domestic animals. As a tribe, it could bring the powers of its men together and wage battle against another tribe. The idea of "Us versus Them" was born and became the basis of ongoing conflicts between human beings. The concept of "winning and losing" and "reward and punishment" came into being.

The evolving mind not only developed tools, but also built weapons to become more powerful than the others. The race to be stronger, to be winners and not losers became a never ending race. The results are pretty obvious! Greed, agitation, restlessness, anger, grievances, hate, revenge, prejudice, sadness, jealousy, fear, anxiety and depression are all by-products of the evolving human mind. And therefore, *it really is the fault of no one.* It is a collective human affliction: the price we pay for the evolution of our mind.

Past and Future

Initially the evolving mind took mental pictures of events that caused it harm: fire burns the hand or a snake bite can kill you. The mind stored these events in order to sense danger and stay away from it.

But with evolution, the human thinking mind simply got out of hand. It evolved into an ever busy machine that continuously takes snapshots of events, attaches a story to them, judges them with information and concepts already stored (*good* or *bad*), which triggers corresponding emotions. The entire bundle of snapshots, story, judging and emotion is then stored as the "*past*." From this past then arise some more thoughts which it calls the "*future.*"

Living in the past and future creates a huge amount of stress as we discussed earlier in this book.

3. Logic

It may appear that we don't have any say in what our "conditioned, conceptual thinking mind" is doing, but that's not true. As a result of evolution, we humans also developed a priceless talent and that is our *logic*. Animals don't have it. Logic is our best asset! By using logic, we can rise above our conceptual, conditioned, thinking mind, bring it under our control and utilize it when necessary. It is only when we are enslaved by the "conceptual, conditioned, thinking mind," that it creates huge stress for us and others.

A Word of Caution:

When I use the word logic, I do not mean rationalization, intellectualization, analysis or interpretation. All of which are actually part of the conditioned mind. By logic, I mean *simple common sense* that every human is born with. You don't learn it. Beware! There is also another kind of common sense that is learned and is based on concepts, and in fact, is a component of the conditioned mind.

Q: What is intelligence? Isn't thinking and intelligence one and the same thing?

A: Thinking and intelligence are *not* one and the same thing. Thinking is only a fraction of the vast intelligence that resides in us. This vast intelligence resides in each and every cell in our body. For example, every cell knows how to replicate itself, when to replicate and how to perform the precise functions that has been assigned to it. For example, some cells produce insulin, some pump blood, some produce digestive enzymes. Each one of these functions requires an incredible amount of intelligence.

In addition, all the cells in the body communicate with each other constantly. For example, the pituitary gland in the brain senses if the amount of thyroid hormone produced by the

288

thyroid gland is just right, too low or too high. Then it sends its feedback to the thyroid gland by producing a hormone, we call TSH (Thyroid Stimulating Hormone). In this way the pituitary gland regulates the production of thyroid hormone by the thyroid gland. This is just one example how various parts of the body interact with each other. There is unbelievable *interaction, communication* and *harmony* between various organs of the body - all working together for the welfare of the whole organism. This is just scratching the surface about this *universal intelligence* residing in our body. A full description of this intelligence is certainly beyond the scope of this book. It would require several volumes and perhaps still not be fully described.

Suffice is to say that the intelligence that resides in us knows no boundaries. "Thinking" only represents a tiny fraction of our intelligence.

Q: Isn't the mind doing what it's supposed to be doing?

A: On the surface, it's true that the mind is doing what it's supposed to do. It's pretty obvious that in its doing, it creates a huge amount of stress for itself and also for everyone else. But it is the *conditioned mind*. And it is doing what it has been programmed to do, just like a computer or a robot.

Chapter 38

Freedom from the Conceptual World

There is a conceptual world, in your head, your Acquired Self, created by the collective conceptual world of humans. Both are virtual, unreal, illusory. With few exceptions, every person on the planet stays in the prison of their conceptual world. *As long as you are in the conceptual world, you will experience stress, in one form or another.*

In order to be free of stress, you need to be free of the conceptual world. But how? If you want to be free of concepts, you first have to understand the true nature of concepts. Use logic and you realize that *concepts are not reality and reality is not conceptual.*

You acquire concepts from the conceptual world of the society you grow up in. They become part of your Acquired Self. *You are not born with these concepts.* With this realization, you are immediately free of these concepts. You rise above them. You are no longer attached to concepts. *You neither love them nor hate them.* You see them exactly for what they are. You see their *relative functionality* when interacting in the conceptual world. However, you do not get overtaken by them or start believing in them as the absolute truth.

For example, you use money to buy a car, but you don't get attached to the concept of "My car." It is a car that you can use to go from point "A" to point "B." That's all. Because there is no "Me," you have no need to enhance your ego by spending a large sum of money on a prestigious name car.

You understand the whole concept of "money and trading" to function in society and that's all. You don't believe in "My car." You don't get any ego enhancement through "My car."

In the same way, you can buy a house, but it doesn't become "My house." You simply have done some trading so that you have shelter. Tomorrow, you can sell it to someone else. That's all. You don't believe that your house is more than bricks, wood and cement. You don't seek any ego enhancement through "My house."

You get married to live according to the rules of society, but you also understand that suddenly you don't own "My wife." You continue to see her as another human being.

You also use language to talk to other humans, but you don't believe in the concepts attached to words. You understand what concepts are attached to words, but you don't believe in them as absolute truth.

Practice:

You can be free of the conceptual world right Now!

Please close the book, and get a pen and paper. Write down *"who you think you are."* Be honest. You won't share this information with anyone and afterwards, you should shred this piece of paper. You may end up writing something like this:

I am Paul Brown.
I am a Christian.
I am a Canadian.
I am an attorney.
I am a father.
I am in a relationship which unfortunately is not working out for me.
I do not want to hurt others feelings.
I own a house.
I own a car.
I am a successful person.
I am member of a club, called -------.
I believe in----------------.
I made many mistakes in the past, which I regret now.
I am striving for a bright future.
I am an honest, hardworking person.
I do not like those who lie or cheat.
I am not a racist person.
I want world peace.
I love Canada.
I am worried about global warming and want to save the earth.
I hate those who hate Canada.
I am doing everything possible to prevent cancer, heart attack, Alzheimer's dementia, etc.

I miss my mother who passed away last year.
I do not want to suffer the way she did from her disabilities.
I love pets.
I love sports.
I hate cold weather.
I hate long hours at work.
I resent my greedy, demanding boss.
I wish people were nicer.
I do not get all the appreciation that I deserve.
I have a lot of friends on the internet.
I love Christmas.
I do not like those who fart in public and don't even say "excuse me."
I have a good knowledge of history.
I love to spend my vacation in Hawaii.
I don't like my grey hair.
I don't like getting old.
I can never be on time.
I hate it when someone complains about me.
I hate it when people are impatient, loud and insensitive.
I don't like to be pushed around.
When necessary, I can be very tough.
I love rock and roll music.
I love the internet.
I love watching football games with my friends while drinking beer.
I hate to be alone.
I am a strong, sensitive, drug-free, disease free, middle age man.
I love to party.

And the description may go on and on.

Now use logic and you'll realize all of these descriptions actually refer to various components of the virtual, conceptual world in your head. The virtual "I" stays lost in the conceptual, virtual world and suffers from endless stress, which it blames on others and at times, on itself.

With this realization, you will be instantaneously free of the conceptual world in your head. Then you will be able to see things more clearly.

The Real "I" versus the Virtual "I"

The real "I" is <u>real</u> and hence needs no description. Any description is always conceptual because language itself is conceptual.

Suffice it to say that It is the real "I" that:
- Sees
- Hears
- Smells
- Tastes
- Feels the touch, vibration, temperature and energy flowing throughout the body
- Makes sounds
- Lies down, sits, stands and moves

Everything it does is real.

On the other hand, the virtual "I" consists of ideas, concepts, information, knowledge, the past, the future, emotions and has a lengthy description, as we observed earlier. *It is virtual and stays in the virtual, conceptual world.*

When you are free of the Virtual "I," you spontaneously get in touch with your Real "I," which instantaneously puts you in the "NOW," where there is no stress whatsoever.

Q: How can I Live in This World Without Concepts?

A: If you use logic, you realize that concepts are concepts, nothing more. They are not real.

With this realization, you are free of concepts. Once you rise above concepts, life gets simple and stress free without even trying. *Then you utilize concepts to live in the conceptual world, but you are not in the grip of these concepts.*

For example, you make money just to purchase necessary commodities: food, house, clothes, car, etc. That's all. You don't have to pay large sums of money for some prestigious name attached to your car, shirts or shoes. You don't need to purchase items of luxury, ego-enhancement or entertainment. You don't need to have money for a flashy lifestyle. You don't have the psychological rope of friends and enemies around your neck. You live a simple, basic life. The stress of "coming up with money to pay for your lifestyle" automatically disappears.

On the other hand, if you try to live a simple life as a concept, you'll feel miserable because you are in the grip of all sorts of concepts. You will constantly be asking, "Why should I live a simple life?" You'll find plenty of concepts that will justify living a simple life and plenty of concepts that will justify *not* living a simple life. *Remember, a concept can never liberate you from concepts.* It simply adds to the pile of concepts and concepts are an important component of your Acquired Self. Enslaved in the Acquired Self, you never see your True Self!

Chapter 39

Practical Living

To live in the conceptual civilized world and stay free of your Acquired Self is quite challenging. The conceptual world has an enormous pull on you. After all, you've been trapped in the conceptual world for a very long time and are very used to it, even though it creates all kind of stress for you.

Therefore, it's important to minimize the conceptual world to bare necessities. Then, you will have plenty of time to stay in the real world, the Now. It is helpful to pay attention to the following points while you continue to live in the conceptual world.

Figure out What is Necessary and What is Unnecessary

While in the grip of the Acquired Self, you stay in a rut without ever logically looking at what is necessary and what is unnecessary. For example, if you feel that you don't have time, isn't it logical to look at where your time goes?

A majority of people spend a lot of their time in activities which are unnecessary, such as watching TV, reading newspapers and magazines, surfing on the internet, text messaging and gossiping on the phone. "But everyone else is into these things. Who will I be without these activities?" says your

Acquired Self. Yes, 99% of the population is into these activities and is lost in the conceptual world. That's why there is so much stress.

To blend in and desire to be accepted is an activity of the Acquired Self. If you decide to engage in all these activities and find that you have no time left, then please don't complain about it. You have decided to spend all your time doing what everyone else is doing and that's all. Just see it the way it is. Certain activities are obviously necessary. For example, your job, driving your kids to school, preparing meals.

Isn't it is important to dissect out what is necessary from what is not?

If you look deeply, you realize that everyone has some basic necessities of life such as food, shelter, clothing. Beyond these basic necessities, everyone has their own individual activities as a product of their Acquired Self and the conceptual world they live in. People confuse these activities as necessities. These activities constitute your lifestyle, not your life necessities.

The more you are in the grip of the Acquired Self, the more important these activities appear to be and even may feel like necessities of life. These activities vary from person to person, depending on the composition of their Acquired Self and the conceptual world they live in.

These activities of the Acquired Self have a lot in

300

common for people living in a certain conceptual world created by a certain cultural, religious and geo-political environment.

Many of these activities center around convenience - the convenience of modern living. For example, cell phones, computers, electricity, air-conditioning, central heating, airplanes, cars, etc.

Many activities center around entertainment such as TV, magazines, internet, video games and movies. Not too long ago, people lived without these activities of convenience and entertainment, a fact many people seem to have forgotten.

Most people get lost in these activities and start to *seek themselves* in these activities. It is basically their ego (I, Me, My, Mine), which is the core of the Acquired Self. For example, they may consider themselves to be a cultured, high class person if they go to see stage shows, museums and belong to a certain club. Others feel special if they attend a certain sports event, concert or political rally.

Even basic necessities of life can become part of "I, Me, My, Mine." People spend a lot of money in order to enhance their ego.

For example, they seek themselves in designer clothes, exclusive communities and eating at certain famous, expensive restaurants. In order to keep this expensive lifestyle, they also have to produce a high income, which in most cases means they have to spend many hours working. Then, they complain about not having any time.

Many also get a lot of stress from the nature of their work. Some don't even like their work, but keep doing because it pays for their lifestyle. Even the thought of losing their income creates huge stress. If they do lose their income, they have a tremendous amount of stress. Life seems meaningless. Many become depressed and even suicidal.

So What's the Solution?

You need to sit down and figure out for yourself what truly are the basic necessities of life and what activities are important for your Acquired Self, but otherwise are not *necessities*.

Watch out for the activities that enhance your sense of the Acquired Self, the self-image, the ego. With this awareness, you won't have the compulsion to choose these activities as necessities of life. You do these activities if time and money permits and enjoy them while doing them instead of being stressed out. If you can't do them for whatever reason, then you won't be stressed out either.

Practical Wisdom:

Practical wisdom goes like this: Find some work that you like to do. Do it just to make a living. Don't get addicted to it. *Then let your income dictate your expenses.* Don't seek yourself

302

through your possessions or life-style. Watch out when "wanting more" creeps into your head. Don't let it overtake you. There will be no stress while you make your daily living. This is in sharp contrast to what most people who are totally stressed out do these days. They go and buy things on credit and then they have to come up with income to cover the expenses. The amount of work as well as the sword of credit debt creates huge stresses for these people.

Step 3

Live in the Now

Chapter 40

Live in the Now

You may have heard "live in the Now" and you won't have any stress. Well, it is true that there is no stress in the Now. Then, why don't you live in the Now?

What Prevents You From Living in the Now?

Pay attention and you clearly see it's your busy mind that prevents you from living in the Now. As long as you're in the grip of the busy mind, you are not in the "Now." "Living in the busy mind" and "Living in the Now" are mutually exclusive.

In order to live in the "Now," you need to be free of your busy mind. In order to be free of your busy mind, you need to look at the dynamics of your busy mind. Observe your busy mind and you'll see that it's lost in the past or the future. It tells stories of the past, promises or fears of the future, talks about concepts and points of view. It judges itself and others. Often, it talks to imaginary people, expressing its anger, frustrations and concerns even when no one else is there. That's how your mind stays busy.

The Busy Mind consists of your *past, future, concepts, ideas, knowledge and information* that you acquire from society as you grow up. It's your Acquired Self, isn't it? In other words, it is your Acquired Self that keeps your mind busy and thus, prevents you from living in the Now.

Your Acquired Self keeps you in the past and or in the future. Why? Because it is the one who creates the past and future, otherwise they do not exist. The past and future are virtual, created by your Acquired Self who itself is virtual. So your Acquired Self resides in its self-created home of the *past* and *future*.

Your Acquired Self keeps you in the world of concepts, ideas, beliefs, points of view, judgments, interpretations and labels. Why? Because these are various components of your Acquired Self. As long as you are identified with your Acquired Self, you stay in its grip.

On the other hand, your True Self is real and lives in the Now, which is Real. In the Now, there is no emotional burden of the past or worries of the future. In the Now, there are no concepts, no ideas, no beliefs, no customs, no traditions. *In the Now, everything is real.* The Present Moment is always fresh, pristine and without any stress. Therefore, live in the now and be free of all of the stress created by your Acquired Self. To live in the Now, be free of your Acquired Self.

CAUTION!
Your Acquired Self loves to acquire more and more concepts. "Living in the Now" often becomes a concept. It simply adds to your Acquired Self and in this way keeps you away from living in

the Now. Ironic! The more you remain in the concept of "living in the Now: the more you will be away from the "Now."

Don't make living in the Now a goal. That is what your Acquired Self loves to do. In this way, it creates a future and therefore, keeps you out of the present moment. The Acquired Self is very treacherous!

Live in Your "Field of Awareness"

So, how do you live in the present moment?

We are equipped with five senses. *Sight, sound, smell, taste and touch.* These five senses create an *outer field of awareness* for you.

Live in your Outer Field of Awareness

Pause for a moment right now and pay attention to what you see, what you hear; what you smell, what you taste and what you touch. Don't think, just observe. Experience what's in your field of awareness.

In general, when we see, we only pay attention to objects without paying any attention to the *space* in which everything is. Without space, there would be no objects. So when you see objects, also be aware of the space which gives rise to all the objects in the universe.

In the same way, when you listen, also pay attention to the *silence* without which there would be no sound.

Use your eyes and ears and be aware of *space, silence* and *stillness*, which is the background in which all objects exist, all sounds arise and all events take place.

- Without space there would be no objects.
- Without silence there would be no sound.
- Without stillness there would be no events.

Live in your Inner Field of Awareness:

In addition to your outer field of awareness, you also have an *inner field of awareness* that you can access by paying attention to it.

This inner field of awareness is your *original, True Self.* It is vibrant, full of immense energy, joy and inner peace. No words can accurately describe it, but it can be felt. It is an experience and not a concept. That's why your Acquired Self, which consists of concepts, cannot understand it. You can feel your inner field of awareness simply by calming your busy mind and taking your attention inside you.

In fact, your outer field of awareness is an extension of your inner field of awareness. It is one field of awareness. And that is what the Now is!

Q: How Can I live in the Now, if my Present is Awful?

A: This is a wonderful way for your Acquired Self to rationalize why you shouldn't live in the now. In this way, it keeps you enslaved.

Pay attention and you realize that there is a "conceptual present" that your conditioned mind, your Acquired Self creates. In this conceptual present, you may find a lot of undesirable things such as lack of money, lack of health, lack of a romantic relationship, etc. Of course, this conceptual present may be awful and you want to run away from it by escaping into a fantasy land, called the future: this is the basis of *hope*.

However, when I refer to the Now or Present, I am referring to the Now in Real; *not a concept, but a reality-* the reality of what you actually see, hear, smell, taste, touch and feel. Stay in this real "Now" without any *interference* from your conditioned, busy mind. Be aware that your conditioned mind loves to *interpret*, *judge* and *conceptualize* everything that it sees, hears, smells, touches, tastes or feels. For example, you see a sunset. For a moment you are in awe (the real present), but the next moment your conditioned mind hijacks your attention and you find yourself interpreting, comparing, describing or even taking a picture of the sunset. All of these mental activities create a "conceptual present" for you. You are no longer in the real Now.

In the real Now, there is never ever any stress! The real Now is not a concept. It is reality around and inside you and you

309

can be aware of it any time you decide. It is your ultimate choice! Unfortunately, most people are not even aware of this ultimate choice and therefore, continue to suffer in the virtual land of the *past* and *future*, which is a part of their conditioned mind, their Acquired Self.

Chapter 41

How to Live in the Now in Real Life

Your Acquired Self, the conditioned mind, keeps you away from the *Now*, because the *Now* is *real* and your Acquired Self is *unreal*. Your Acquired Self creates an *unreal, virtual, conceptual* world of its own and keeps you trapped there. The past and future are part of this virtual world.

Because your Acquired Self has been in the driver's seat since your early childhood, you keep going back to your past and future, despite trying to stay in the *Now*. Here are some practical suggestions for how to spend more and more time in the *Now*.

Keep Your Mind Where Your Body Is

If you pay attention, you realize that your mind is almost always out of sync with your body. While your body sits in the car as you travel along a road, your mind may be miles and years away remembering what you did on your last vacation. Maybe you're still trying to win the argument you had with your colleague a week ago. If you have the radio on, it further facilitates your mind's tendency to wander into the conceptual world, away from the present moment.

This ever busy mind is the dysfunction of the human

mind. It is your Acquired Self, the Monster that keeps you either in the past or the future, both of which are unreal. It keeps you away from reality, the present moment.

Now you have to ask yourself, is it possible to keep your mind in the present moment? And what is the present moment? For you, the present moment is where your body is. So, if you can keep your mind where your body is, you will be in the Now.

For example, if you are driving, keep your mind on the road. Pay attention to the other traffic, the trees, electricity poles running backward, the clouds swirling in the sky, the birds, the buildings and everything else you see or hear. While walking through the parking lot, pay attention to the warm or cold air and everything that you see and hear.

When you're at work, pay attention to whatever you are doing at work. No gossiping, reading magazines or playing on the internet. When you are at home, keep your mind at home by paying attention to everything that you do or whatever is happening around you. While you eat, pay attention to your food and taste every bite of it. Pay attention to your surroundings. Pay attention to the texture of the chair you are sitting on.

No thinking about what happened at work or what is happening next week, etc.; Be aware of this tendency of your mind to stay in the past or jump into the future. Each time you see it away from the present moment, gently bring it back to the present moment - the physical surroundings where your body is.

Just keep your mind where your body is by paying attention to your five senses. Sometimes, also pay attention to your breathing, which is an act in the present moment.

That's how you live in the Now, the present moment, the reality.

Frequently Ask Yourself These Two Questions

1. Is it happening right now, at this very moment, in reality?

Almost always the answer will be "NO." The thoughts in your head often create a picture which seems very real, but in fact is virtual, an illusion in your head. For it to be real, you should be able to sense it with any of your five senses.

2. Let's see what is happening right now.

Use your five senses to observe what is happening right now, in reality.

Beware of Your Acquired Self

Your busy mind, the Acquired Self is very treacherous and will try to trick you into its own virtual world. It will do every thing possible to keep you away from the *Now*. It may creep in as an inner voice like, "easier said than done," *Or* "It makes sense, but it's so hard to do."

With these kinds of comments, your Acquired Self is coming up with a clever *excuse* for not changing your old habits and that's how it keeps you trapped.

Now use logic and ask yourself, "How hard can it be to be mentally present where you are physically present?" It is so logical and so easy. Initially, your busy mind keeps pulling you back into its grip and you wander off into the past and future and that's OK. Simply observe this activity of the Acquired Self and move on to the present moment. That's all. Stay alert and beware of your Acquired Self.

Q: I get so frustrated that I still can't control my mind. What should I do?

A: You get frustrated because you have set a goal of controlling your mind. Whenever you have a goal, you have built-in expectations and you are doomed to be frustrated. Setting up goals is an activity of the Acquired Self, a habit that you learn as a result of psycho-social conditioning. *If you have no goal, then there is no frustration.* Please don't make "living in the Now and watching your Acquired Self" a goal that you will achieve one day.

Also, it's not about *controlling your mind.* It's about *paying attention* to your mind without condemning it. It is simply observing your mind. *Control* of any sort is an activity of your Acquired Self.

314

You simply keep your mind in the physical surroundings of your body and that's all. Often, you find that your mind has wandered off and that's OK. You simply realize it and bring it back to the present surroundings. You don't judge or condemn your self. *Judging* is another trick your Acquired Self loves to play. It may say, "See, you can't do this. It's so hard. You failed again. You didn't achieve what you were supposed to. You're not good enough. You need special training for this. Maybe you need to find a teacher, a guru or attend a workshop."

Be aware of all the tricks your Acquired Self plays. Observe your Acquired Self in action as an inner voice. Just observing it will free you of it.

Q: But Living in The Now May Affect My Abilities.

A: Yes, living in the Now, indeed affects your abilities, but in a positive way. When you pay attention to whatever you're doing, you get better at it, even though you're not trying to get better. Amazing!

For example, you don't forget where you placed something and no longer lose time or your temper trying to find misplaced items. You also learn faster and you finish your task in less time. Actually, you become more proficient and more productive.

315

I know I have become a better driver, a better doctor, a better boss, a better husband and a better father. However, please don't make it a goal. It happens automatically.

You may be surprised to find some of your hidden talents. Until a few years ago, I had no idea that I could be a painter, a gardener, a cook, a writer and a poet. These talents simply sprung up after I started "living in the now" and these give me a lot of joy. Now, instead of wasting a lot of time watching TV, reading newspapers, surfing on the internet and gossiping on the telephone, which I used to do before, I simply keep my mind where my body is. It has freed up a lot of time that I used to waste before. I never feel rushed. I enjoy whatever I am doing in the present moment. Living this way is so much fun and full of joy, but it cannot be put into words. You have to live it for yourself.

Just Do It and Don't Give Up

Just start living in the Now right away. Don't think why, how and when you will be comfortable with the idea of living in the Now. These are clever hindrances your Acquired Self puts forward, in order to keep you in its trap.

When you live in Now, even for a moment, you are free from the emotional burden of the past and the anxieties of the future. In that moment, you experience inner peace and joy.

As you recall from earlier chapters, your mind creates the past and future for you and then it lives in it. The more it stays in the past and the future, the less it stays in the present. The reverse is also true. The more it stays in the present, the less it stays in the past and the future. The past and future are store houses for all your stress. Living in the past creates frustrations, anger, bitterness, revenge, grievances, jealousy, worthlessness, shame and depression. Living in the future creates fear, restlessness, insomnia, anxiety and panic attacks. Most people live in the past and the future most of the time and that's why they have so much stress in their life.

When you start living in the Now, you will immediately find relief from stress. A moment later, you might return to the grip of the past and the future and their associated stress. A few minutes later, you may become aware that you were lost in the past and the future. With this awareness, you return back to the Now. You go back and forth between living in the present and living in the past and the future. As you continue to live this way, you spend more and more time in the Now and less and less time in the past and the future.

The mind in the present moment is quiet, calm, sharp, fresh and observing. The mind in the past and the future is noisy, chattering, judging, repetitive, machine-like, tired and dull.

Chapter 42

Meditation

Meditation is a great way to calm your busy mind. Every day, spare at least 15 minutes in the morning and 15 minutes in the evening to do some meditation. Morning meditation prepares you to start your day with a relaxed mind. Evening meditation helps you to wash away all the emotional burdens you may have collected during the day. It also prepares you for a restful sleep.

The Art of Meditation

You can do meditation in a sitting position or a lying down position: whatever is comfortable for you. For most people, sitting in a chair works well. If you are more flexible, then you can sit on a mat in a more traditional lotus or half lotus position with your legs crisscross.

There are several types of meditation. You can do them together in sequence or separately.

Be in a quiet area away from phones and other noises. No music please.

Sit or lay comfortably. Close your eyes.

Body Meditation:

Pay attention to your body parts, starting with your feet. Feel the weight, pressure and sensation in your feet. Now move your attention to your legs, knees, thighs and pelvic area. Mentally feel each area for a minute or two. Then move onto the lower back, middle back, and upper back. Stretch your entire back with your imagination. Then focus on your neck and skull. Then bring your attention to your face. Soften the muscles and come down to the neck, arms, chest and abdomen, spending few minutes at each area, mentally feeling and softening each area.

Breathing Meditation:

Bring your attention to your breathing. Observe how your chest expands with each inhalation and retracts with each exhalation. Just feel the movement of your chest. Stay focused on the movement of your chest.

No thinking, but just pay attention to your breath and the energy flowing inside your body. If your mind runs away with some thought, do not get upset. As soon as you realize that your attention was distracted, bring it back to the movement of your chest with each breath. Your chest movement becomes the anchor of your attention.

Initially, you will find that your mind is as busy as a bee, but gradually, it starts to calm down. You gradually start to feel a pleasant *spacious* feeling in your chest. You may also see some shapes, usually purple colored, in front of your closed eyes. Don't get involved. Stay focused on your chest movements and *spacious* feeling in your chest. Every now and then you feel intense vibrant sensations running throughout your body. Again, just experience them, but do not get attached. Get back to the movement of your chest.

After a few minutes, pay attention to the *energy* running through your body. Observe how with each inhalation, this energy rises up from the base of your spine to the top of your head. And with each exhalation, it flows down into your chest and abdomen.

Continue to be the observer, paying attention to all that's happening in your body. You may be amazed to discover the *energy*, *joy* and *peace* that you never experienced before.

Walking Meditation:

As you get tired of sitting, get up and start walking. Pay attention to each step. Realize how the right arm and left leg move forward and backward together (and the left arm and right leg move forward and backward together).

To keep it simple, just pay attention to one set of arm and leg. I use the right arm and left leg. Also, pay attention to your breathing, the space in which your body is moving forward. You can sense the walls of the corridor moving backward, if you are walking in a corridor, of course.

321

Meditation All the Time:

Keep your mind where your body is. Then you meditate while carrying on your daily activities. While driving, pay attention to space and everything in it: electricity poles, traffic, trees, birds, sky, clouds, etc. In the parking lot, pay attention to space and everything in it: other cars, curbs, concrete, signs, etc. In your office, be aware of space and everything in it: desk, computer, chair, walls, people, etc. In the grocery store, be aware of space and everything in it: the aisles, items on the shelf, people, carts, lines, clerks, machines, etc. In a restaurant, pay attention to space and everything in it: chairs, tables, items on the table including your food, walls, people, etc.

Every now and then, also pay attention to your breath. Feel how with each inhalation, energy rises from the base of your spine to the top of your spine and then into your head. With each exhalation, energy flows down from your head into your chest and abdomen. You may be sitting alone in a restaurant or driving your car and feeling peaceful and joyful with this energy flowing up and down your body. It is such a great feeling. Words cannot describe it. You have to experience it yourself.

Imagine, next time you are in a traffic jam or in a line at the airport or grocery store, you will be joyful and peaceful in your meditative state, instead of being stressed out. This is the key to stress-free living.

322

Meditation in a Social Setting:

It is relatively easy to stay in the meditative state while you are alone, even if you are in a social setting, such as eating alone at a restaurant or waiting in a line. But it is quite challenging when you are in company and you have to participate in a conversation. As soon as you engage in conversation, you easily get taken over by your Acquired Self. Then, you are not in the Now.

However, you can master the art of paying attention to your surroundings, the space around you, and carry on a conversation. It is useful to remember to come to a *full stop* after expressing your opinion and to know that it is your opinion, not the ultimate truth. You don't need to defend it. Every now and then, you will be taken over by your Acquired Self, but soon you will realize it and get out of its grip.

Meditation Can Enlighten You

After a few sessions of meditation, you may start to re-experience your past experiences. This time, see them as an observer. See how your Acquired Self and Acquired Selves of others were at each others throats in those experiences. Do not judge. Just observe.

Then, you may have a new realization about your past experiences. For example, in the past, you got upset with your brother, a friend or a parent who let you down. They did not behave in the manner that your Acquired Self wanted. You carry all of that psychological pain with you all the time. Imagine over your life time, how many times others, especially the one you had expectations from, let you down and caused emotional pains. Imagine the amount of pain you are carrying.

Can you fully realize that your relatives or friends did not meet the expectations of your Acquired Self? It's your Acquired Self who is hurting and holding on to all the pain and bitterness. Only once you fully realize it, can you let go of it. You will truly be amazed how transforming this experience can be. You feel a huge weight lift off your chest. This is true forgiveness with tremendous healing power.

Compare it to the usual concept of forgiveness: You forgive someone because you're a better person or you must forgive, otherwise you will be punished. This actually nourishes your Acquired Self and that's why it has no real healing potential.

Chapter 43

Dealing with Stressful Situations

Most people stay in the grip of their Acquired Self, which torments them constantly, creating inner stress even when there is no *stressful situation*.

In life, sooner or later, one faces a stressful situation, which we can call **outer stress**. Already up to their neck due to ongoing **inner stress**, most people overreact to the outer stressful situation, creating more stress for themselves and for others.

For example, you may call for tech support help for your computer and get a representative who speaks with a foreign accent. This tech support helper may very well be physically sitting in an office in a foreign country. If you (actually your Acquired Self) already dislikes foreigners for one reason or other, you have little patience with this person on the other side of the phone, who with her little training tries to help you. You may find yourself bursting into a *rage* at her, which of course makes matters worse. The tech support helper may hang up on you or may be so terrified by your temper, that she becomes even less effective in solving your problem. Later, you may tell your version of the story to your friends who probably agree with your action and this validation further strengthens your Acquired Self. While telling the story, you experience *hate* and *anger* again and actually cause harm to your own health.

So What's the Solution?

There is another way to handle stressful situations, which actually turns out to be more effective in solving the problem and does not produce stress for you or the other person.

In the above mentioned example, someone who already has some insight into his Acquired Self may see the "Monster" of *prejudice* and *hate* rising inside him before he starts to yell. Maybe he realizes in the middle of his yelling, that it is his "Monster" who has taken over. Seeing the "Monster" is enough. As soon as you can see it, it does not hold control over you. Free of the "Monster," this person clearly sees what's happening. He may find himself saying, "Sorry, it's nothing personal, but I'm just tired of waiting such a long time on the phone, but I do appreciate you trying to help me." The person on the other side may go the extra mile and being free of stress, will be more capable of finding the solution.

When you're out of the grip of your Monster, you actually communicate in a much more effective manner and get much better results. When you are not emotionally charged, you can actually think clearly and say exactly what the problem is. Chances are that you or your helper will be able to find the answer.

Once you are free of your Acquired Self, your inner stress dissipates and you don't overreact to stressful situations.

Often, your Acquired Self takes you back in its prison before you know it. You start to overreact to a situation, but soon you realize that your Monster took over and caused you to act the way you did. This realization has a transforming effect. You may find yourself apologizing to your spouse, your child or your employee, much to their surprise. Each time you see the Monster in action, even if you see it after the fact, it loosens its grip on you.

When you are not in the grip of your Acquired Self, you also start to live in a practical way, which tremendously reduces the magnitude of your outer stress. You are able to look at any stressful situation with logic, without any emotional overreaction.

For example, you lose your job for one reason or another and face a financial situation. If you already live in a practical way, chances are that you won't have heavy debts. You will be free of the heavy monthly expenses that most people incur these days. You further reduce your expenses as your income drops. Thinking logically, you look at your options and take action if necessary.

Most Situations are Actually Not Stressful at All!

Use logic and you will see that all stress comes from the conceptual world in your head, your Acquired Self. When you are consumed by the conceptual world, you constantly face stressful situations. On the other hand, when you rise above the conceptual world, the stressful situation is not stressful any longer.

For example:

Traffic jams and all of the resulting stress is a product of the civilized, conceptual world, isn't it? Most people experience this stress every day. Is it possible not to experience the stress of heavy traffic? In the grip of the conceptual world in your head, (which is your Acquired Self), you say, "No. The stress due to traffic is part of life and you have to live with this stress." This thinking gives rise to an underlying emotion of *helplessness*. However, once you are free of the conceptual world in your head, your Acquired Self, you no longer experience the stress due to traffic jams.

Example:

A man in the total grip of his Acquired Self gets into a traffic jam while driving to the airport. His Acquired Self torments him with the fear of missing the flight and all the consequences that may happen if he misses the flight. He soon starts blaming his wife for being late. "Had you not.........., we wouldn't be in this mess." Of course, his wife's Acquired Self strikes back with some defensive comment, "It's all your fault and you're blaming me? How dare you?!! You always do that. I'm sick of your behavior." This war between the two monsters goes on, verbally or silently, until they arrive at the airport. Of course, both are totally stressed out and if anything else goes wrong, he will get into a rage and create a scene.

Now consider another driver, who has some freedom from his Acquired Self. He sees his Monster of fear and anger rising, but will not get lost in its grip. He uses logic and looks at his choices. "I cannot leave this situation, I cannot change this situation, so I should better accept it the way it is, drive carefully and not get in an accident." If he also remembers to "keep your mind where your body is," he will pay attention to his surroundings, space and everything in it. He will also pay attention to his breathing and feel the energy flowing in his body. This driver arrives at the airport at the same time as the first driver, but without any stress whatsoever. Actually, he will be in a meditative state, full of peace, joy and energy. In the very same situation, one person collected and distributed a lot stress. In contrast, the other person dealt with it without any stress.

Therefore, it is very important for you to be free of your Acquired Self even when there are no stressful situations. And put *meditation at all times* into practice. Then, at the time of "stressful situations," you will not overreact. You will deal with the situation while remaining peaceful, joyful and full of energy. Only then, you realize that most situations are not stressful at all.

Practical Steps to Handle a Stressful Situation

Next time you're faced with a stressful situation, try to follow these steps. Be still and bring your mind in the Now, the

329

present moment. Observe your field of awareness by looking, hearing, smelling, touching and tasting. Pay attention to your breathing. Count your breaths.

Then, you will be able to observe your Acquired Self reacting to the situation. Be aware of the thoughts running through your head: *What if, What may*, etc.; Realize these are just thoughts, that's all. What they imply is not real, because it is not happening at this very moment. Then see what your options are. Ask yourself:

1. Is there a need for action?

Often there is *no* need for action. For example, you're driving on the freeway and someone cuts right in front of you, even without turning his car blinker light on. If you are in the grip of your Acquired Self, you may react almost instantaneously, as a knee jerk reflex. You may honk at the other driver, give him a finger, shout some curse words, etc.; Your Monster of *competition* and *self-righteousness* is in full action. In a fast mode, it is thinking like this: "That guy got ahead. I got behind. He won and I lost. He is a bad guy who didn't follow the rules." Your Monster decides to fight back and takes an action that creates a huge amount of stress for you as well as the other driver, who may decide to fight back. This is the basis of *road rage*.

However, if you are free from your Acquired Self, you clearly see it's the other driver's monster in action. You see how it invites your Monster to engage. You simply keep driving as if nothing happened. No stress for you and no stress for the other driver. You did not take any action at all and effectively prevented a stressful situation.

2. Sometimes you need to take action:

There are occasions when action may be necessary and you can take action to change the situation.

For example:

- You have medical problems from being overweight. You can change your eating habits.

- You are about to be robbed. You can run.

- You don't like your long work hours and you are self-employed. You can take action by cutting your hours. Of course, this may result in a reduction in your income.

- Your receptionist is rude and unprofessional to your clients and does not change her behavior despite several warnings from you. You can take action and terminate her.

While free from your Acquired Self, actions that you take are not instantaneous reactions of your Monster, but arise out of your True Self. These actions are of high quality and are very effective.

While you live in your True Self, in the Now, the solution to the situation will arise inside you. It will be without any *fear, anger, revenge, bitterness, self-righteousness* or *greed*. In your heart, you will know it is the right thing to do. **In addition, you will not look for certain results.** You will not be attached to the results at all.

On the other hand, actions that arise out of your Acquired Self are tainted by your Acquired Self and are filled with *anger, hate, jealousy, judgment, greed, self-fulfillment* or *fear*. Often, these actions are attached to certain results. For example, I often hear my patients ask, "If I follow what you are telling me, will I lose 15 pounds in two months and will I be able to prevent diabetes?" I tell them, "Just take action. Simply change your eating habits and that's all. Don't be attached to the results."

3. Sometimes you cannot take any action.

In many situations, there is no action that you can take, just as we saw in the example of the traffic jam on the way to the airport. If you cannot take any action, simply realize that. Stay in the present moment and continue to live your life. If you are totally in the Now, there will be no psychological stress for you. While there may be physical distress, there will be no psychological stress.

Chapter 44

You are Ageless

Most people don't like getting old. Why don't people like getting old? Because they don't like all the sufferings that old age brings. This is the usual thought pattern about aging. Let's use logic and take a fresh look at age.

What is Age?

There are two types of age:

1. Psychological/Conceptual age
2. Physical age

1. Psychological/Conceptual Age

When we refer to age, we basically refer to what can be called psychological/conceptual age. It is created by your Acquired Self. Time and age are mental abstractions, concepts created by the human mind.

In nature, events are happening all the time. Every event has a beginning and an ending. For example, there is sunrise. This is the beginning of an event which ends with sunset. This event between sunrise and sunset is marked by *light*. Then

333

another event arises, marked by darkness and then it comes to an end. And this cycle of events keeps repeating.

Creation of Conceptual Calendar

Instead of looking at these events as simply events occurring in the universe, the human mind labels them as *day* and *night*. It has to interpret and label everything, otherwise it feels insecure. Initially, the human mind created these simple concepts of day and night, but then it further chopped day and night into hours, minutes and seconds. It also created concepts of months, years, centuries and millennia. This it calls *calendar*. Various cultures have created various calendars. For example, what is called November 30, 2010 in the western calendar is a completely different date in the Chinese calendar, Indian calendar or Islamic calendar.

Creation of Psychological/Conceptual Age

Then the human mind goes one step further and creates another layer of conceptuality. It applies the conceptual calendar to you. Let me explain how.

Like every other event in the universe, you have a beginning (birth or point A) and an ending (death or point B). Between point A and point B, there is a straight, continuous, unbroken line. However, the Collective Acquired Self of society assigns your *beginning* a conceptual date from the conceptual calendar and creates another concept: **Your Birthday,** which

334

keeps repeating itself every 365 days.

Right from your childhood, you are told that this is a special day for you and special things happen just for you on this day: a birthday party, fun food, gifts, telephone calls, etc. Obviously, your Acquired Self starts to expect special things to happen on that particular day every year. If for some reason you don't get what you expected, you feel sad: "No one loves me" says your Acquired Self.

Then you are also given the concept that every 365 days, on your very special day, you get **older** by one year. *That's how the concept of age is created.*

The Society Acquired Self also downloads the concepts of *bigger kid, teenage, grown-up, middle age* and *old age.* In this way, the Acquired Self divides up your life's one straight line from point A to point B into several segments. It also attaches a concept to each and every segment.

Initially, you can't wait to get older. You *love* the concepts attached to the concepts of older kid, teenage, and grown-up. However, then you *hate* the concepts attached to the concepts of middle age and *especially old* age, because the concept of old age is laden with illnesses, ugly appearance, fragility, memory loss, disabilities, lack of independence, worthlessness, loneliness and death. No wonder most people dread the monster of old age.

2. Physical Age

In the grip of your Acquired Self, you are constantly under stress and a stressed out mind leads to a stressed out body through the mind-body connection, as we observed earlier. Consequently, you suffer from a number of psychological disorders and physical illnesses, all of which have detrimental effects on your body. This is what we can call *physical* aging.

Examples:

- In the grip of sports competitions, you subject your body to a number of physical injuries, which often lead to permanent health conditions such as back pain, arthritis, brain damage, etc.

- To escape from the emotional pains and/or seeking more thrill and excitement, you get addicted to food, alcohol, smoking, illegal drugs, excessive partying, excessive and impulsive sex behavior (with potential for sexually transmitted diseases). Each behavior causes physical damage to your body.

- In the grip of traditional foods and eating habits, you often eat for psychological reasons rather than physiological reasons, which often results in obesity, diabetes, high blood pressure, cancer, heart disease, stroke and dementia, all of which cause serious damage to your body.

- "Worrying" as a result of fear created by the "what if syndrome" leads to autoimmune diseases, such as asthma, colitis, thyroid disease, rheumatoid arthritis, with all of the associated serious damage to your body.

- The fear of skin cancer and the tight rope of modern life style leads to vitamin D deficiency and all of its serious health consequences.

- The Acquired Self gives rise to a number of psychological illnesses, which also cause serious harm to your physical body.

- Every medication, every medical procedure, every surgery has potential side-effects which can cause serious damage to your body.

- In the grip of greed, the Collective Acquired Self of society has created severe environmental health hazards, which contribute to a host of medical illnesses.

Isn't it obvious that what we call age is basically a product of the Acquired Self?

You are Ageless

In reality, there is no such thing as age or time. Hence,

you are *ageless*.

However, you realize this reality once you are free of your Acquired Self. Freed from the torment of the Monster, your body has a sigh of relief and starts to rejuvenate. No more incessant thoughts triggering emotions and releasing excess chemicals and hormones in the body. The process of aging slows down.

Death is a Concept

What the conditioned human mind calls "Death" is actually a concept. Even "Birth" is a concept. Each has serious psychological drama attached to it. There are so many negative concepts attached to the concept of death: miserable death, wrongful death, premature death. In reality, you are either present in the Now as a living form (alive) or *not* present in the Now as a living form (dead). That's all. Even saying that someone is *dying* is illogical, as you are alive until you die.

True Fountain of Youth

Living in the now gives you such joy and energy that words can't describe it. This is the *joy of being* that can only be felt. You feel this peaceful energy running throughout your body and it never gets old. This is the true *fountain of youth*. In this way, many illnesses can be prevented and you truly live to the maximum potential of your body and mind.

Chapter 45

The Choice is Yours

Now you understand that the source of *stress* as well as the source of *joy* resides inside you. The choice is yours! This is the most important choice in your life. Unfortunately, most people are not even aware of this choice. Stuck in the grip of their Acquired Self, they are unaware of this choice. Like everyone else around them, they believe that "*stress is part of life*" and not much can be done about it except for medications or other escapes discussed earlier in the book.

After reading this book, you clearly understand that you are the one who is ultimately in the driver's seat. This is true empowerment and does not arise out of insecurity. You can choose *not to be* in the grip of your Acquired Self. You can choose *to be* your True Self.

Therefore, at any given moment, ask yourself, "Am I in the grip of the Acquired Self? Am I lost in my *thoughts, concepts, emotions, beliefs, past* and *future*?" The moment you realize you have been hijacked by the Acquired Self, you actually are no longer in its total grip. It is only when you are not even aware that you are lost in the Acquired Self that you continue to experience stress.

Awareness is the key. To be aware that you are taken over by the Acquired Self will release you from its prison immediately.

Freed from the Acquired Self, you automatically get in touch with your True Self. You become fully aware of your surroundings by using your *five senses*. You also become aware of the *space* and *stillness* in which every thing is. In the *bliss of Now*, you choose to live. You choose to be in touch with your *inner peace and joy*. You choose to be your *True Self*. This is the ultimate choice! Don't ever forget it.

Start to implement this very important choice in your life right now and be free of stress right away.

Dr. Zaidi's Quotes

- Keep your mind where your body is.

- Your conditioned, busy mind is the root cause of your stress. You are not born with this. You acquire it from your society as you grow up.

- The past and future are mental abstractions, virtual and unreal. The present moment is the only *real* thing. Live in it if you want to live a *real* life.

- Many people live a conditional life. In their mind, certain conditions have to be met before they will start living their life. That day never arrives, because they keep adding more and more conditions and goals.

341

- Excessive thinking about the future is the major reason for fear, anxiety and panic attacks.

- You can only solve a problem if it exists, but your busy mind creates a virtual problem and then it tries to take care of this phantom. How absurd!

- Frustrations arise from expectations, which originate from your conditioned mind.

- Most human interactions are actually based upon "conditioned minds interacting." That's why there is so much stress in our lives.

- You can be free of your conditioned mind simply by observing it in action. Don't hate it or you will make it stronger. Simply observing it is enough.

- Human problems can be solved by humans only.

- Live in your field of awareness, created by your five senses: what you see, hear, taste, smell and touch. If it is not in your field of awareness, it is unreal for you at that moment.

- Keep asking yourself two questions: "Is it happening right now, at this very moment, in my field of awareness?" and "What is happening right now, in my field of awareness?"

- True living is like watching a movie, playing continuously around you and realizing that you are also in the movie.

- Concepts divide human beings and that is the basis of conflict and violence. True freedom from violence lies in freedom from concepts.

- Concept is not reality and reality is not conceptual.

- We all live in a conceptual world and mistakenly, take it for real.

- Reality is all around you and inside you. It cannot be described because language itself is conceptual.

- Age is a concept.

- The source of stress as well as joy lies inside you.

- Make the ultimate choice to be stress-free without any outside help.

- Logic is the ultimate asset we humans have.

- Get rid of the filters created by your conditioned mind. Then, take a fresh look at your life with the lightning rod of *logic*.

Acknowledgements

I sincerely acknowledge my wife, Georgie Huntington Zaidi, for doing in-depth proof reading. On a personal note, I am grateful to share my life journey with such a wonderful person.

I also acknowledge our daughter, Zareena, for being such a delightful and insightful person.

Other Books by Dr. Sarfraz Zaidi

"Power of Vitamin D"

In this book, Dr. Zaidi provides comprehensive, yet very useful information about vitamin D deficiency, its health consequences, its diagnosis and treatment without the risk of toxicity. Dr. Zaidi illustrates important practical points by including real case studies from his clinical practice.

"Take Charge of Your Diabetes"

Insulin resistance is the root cause of diabetes in a majority of people, yet most have not even heard of it. In "Take Charge of Your Diabetes," Dr. Zaidi showcases his ground breaking *5-step strategy* to treat diabetes. Using this approach, Dr. Zaidi's patients achieve an excellent control of diabetes, prevent complications of diabetes and above all, do not end up on insulin shots. Those who have been on insulin for years are able to come off insulin.

Dr. Zaidi's website
www.DoctorZaidi.com